G STREET

F STREET

E STREET

D STREET

C STREET

POSTAL MUSEUM

UNION STATION

M

CONSTITUTION AVENUE

PENNSYLVANIA AVENUE

NEW JERSEY AVENUE

NORTH CAPITOL STREET

MASS

RY

ISON DRIVE

THE CAPITOL

4TH STREET

3RD STREET

MARYLAND AVENUE

JEFFERSON DRIVE

R AND SPACE

AMERICAN INDIAN

INDEPENDENCE AVENUE

M

L'ENFANT PLAZA

SMITHSONIAN MUSEUMS
ON OR NEAR THE NATIONAL MALL

Anacostia Community Museum, National Zoological Park,
and Steven F. Udvar-Hazy Center
are located elsewhere in the Washington, DC, metropolitan area.

OFFICIAL GUIDE TO THE
SMITHSONIAN
FOURTH EDITION

SMITHSONIAN BOOKS
WASHINGTON

Library of Congress
Cataloging-in
Publication Data
Smithsonian Institution.
Official guide to the
Smithsonian.
    p. cm.
ISBN 978-1-58834-542-4

1. Smithsonian
Institution—Guidebooks.
2. Washington (D.C.)—
Guidebooks. 3. New York
(N.Y.)—Guidebooks.
I. Title

Q11 .S3S664 2009
917.5304'4—dc22
2009026696

Printed in China, not at
government expense

20 19 18 17 16   5 4 3 2 1

Published by
Smithsonian Books

Director: Carolyn Gleason

Production Editor:
Christina Wiginton

Editorial Assistant:
Raychel Rapazza

Editor: Jane McAllister

Designed by: Jody Billert,
Design Literate Studio, LLC
and Amber Frid-Jimenez

The following are among
the many individuals who
provided invaluable
assistance in the
preparation of this edition:
Marielba Alvarez, Marcia
Baird-Burris, Bridget Balog,
Jennifer Barton, Abigail
Benson, Laurie Bohlk,
Elizabeth Bugbee, Edward
Burke, Rhys Conlon, Joyce
Connolly, Eduardo Diaz,
Marshall Emery, Barbara
Feininger, Miranda Gale,
James Gordon, Becky
Haberacker, Kathleen
Hanser, Kate Haw, Valeska
Hilbig, Anson Hines, Robert
Koestler, Randall Kremer,
Matthew Larsen, Leonda
Levchuk, Melinda Machado,
Eileen Maxwell, Steven
Monfort, Sabrina Motley,
Meghan Murphy, Konrad Ng,
Stephanie Norby, Elizabeth
O'Brien, Valerie Paul,
Allison Peck, Christine
Pulliam, Courtney Rothbard,
Robert Sacheli, Jennifer
Schommer, Michelle Smith,
Jennifer Zoon.

Photo Credits
David Aaronson, Ernest
Amoroso, Mark Avino,
Mildred Baldwin, Toni Brady,
Chip Clark, Jessie Cohen,
James Colburn, Dennis
Cowley, Steven M.
Cummings, Judy Davis /
Hoachlander Davis
Photography, Harold Dorwin,
Matt Flynn, Katherine
Fogden, Gina Fuentes-
Walker, Gallagher &
Associates, Andrew Garn,
Carmelo Guadagno, Marcos
A. Guerra, Marianne Gurley,
David Heald, Tim Hursley,
Bart Kasten, Franko Khoury,
Walter Larrimore, Robert
Lautman, Eric Long, Ellen
McDermott, Bruce Miller,
James O'Donnell, Ken Pelka,
Dane A. Penland, Charles H.
Phillips, John Polman, Dean
Powell, Susana A. Raab,
Frank A. Rinehart, Howard
Ruby, Carolyn Russo, Victor
Schrager, Francie
Schroeder, Frank G. Speck,
Lee Stalsworth, John
Steiner, Richard Strauss,
Steve Tague, Hugh Talman,
Mark Thiessen, Jenn
Thomas, Jeff Tinsley, John
Tsantes, Rick Vargas, John
White, Rolland White, Roger
Whiteside, Gene Young.

Cover: *Portal Gates* by Albert
Paley (b. 1944), 1974. Renwick Gallery.

Endsheets: Map of
the National Mall by
Amber Frid-Jimenez
with special assistance
from National Capital
Planning Commission

CONTENTS

WELCOME TO THE SMITHSONIAN

Welcome to the Smithsonian! Through our
19 museums and galleries, National Zoo, and
numerous research centers, we offer a wide
variety of exciting, inspiring experiences
for the whole family. Whether you're inter-
ested in art, science, history, or culture,
there is something here for everyone. Your
visit can continue long after you've gone
because, increasingly, we are making our
experts and collections accessible online.
It is now easy and convenient for our conversation to continue.

   For more than 170 years, the Smithsonian
has remained true to its mission, "the
increase and diffusion of knowledge,"
and currently maintains scholarly contacts
or conducts research in nearly 90 countries
around the world. The Smithsonian is
involved in pressing issues of the day in
science, education, and concerns of national
identity. It is a vast enterprise that encompasses — in addition to exhibition halls and
art galleries — laboratories, observatories,

field stations, scientific expeditions, classrooms, performing arts events, publications, affiliate museums, the world's largest traveling exhibition service, a cable television channel, numerous Web sites and blogs, and much more.

The remarkable collections of the Smithsonian are the basis for research, exhibitions, and public programs in art, history, and science. The collections include nearly 138 million artifacts, works of art, and scientific specimens. Among them are objects that speak to our nation's unique inquisitiveness, bold vision, creativity, and courage: Edison's light bulb and Morse's telegraph, the Wright flyer, the Apollo 11 command module *Columbia,* Lewis and Clark's compass, Colin Powell's Desert Storm uniform, Mark Twain's self-portrait, and Oscar the Grouch.

Through its creative staff and collections, the Smithsonian presents the astonishing record of American historical, cultural, and scientific achievement with a scope and depth no other institution in the world can match.

In the pages that follow, you'll find many treasures of the Institution pictured and described.

Through exciting exhibitions, *Smithsonian* magazine, the Smithsonian Channel, blogs, affiliate museums, lectures, and tours, the Smithsonian connects Americans to their heritage. You can contribute to America's ongoing story with your questions and comments, and we invite you to do so.

Enjoy your visit. Please come back often!

Opposite and preceding pages: Entrance to the Castle on the south side, from Independence Avenue and the Enid A. Haupt Garden. Overleaf: Located along the north side of the Arts and Industries Building is the Kathrine Dulin Folger Rose Garden.

Metrorail:
Smithsonian station.
For information about
the Smithsonian, call
202-633-1000
(voice/tape),
e-mail us at
info@si.edu,
or visit si.edu.

Begin your
Smithsonian visit
at the Smithsonian
Visitor Center
in the Smithsonian
Institution Building
(the Castle) on
the National Mall,
open daily, except
December 25, from
8:30 A.M. to 5:30 P.M.

VISITING THE
SMITHSONIAN IN
WASHINGTON, DC

The Smithsonian Institution is a complex of 19 museums, the National Zoological Park, and numerous research facilities. Seventeen museums and the Zoo are located in the Washington, DC, area. The Cooper Hewitt, Smithsonian Design Museum and the National Museum of the American Indian, George Gustav Heye Center are in New York City.

Here is some basic information to help you plan your Smithsonian visit.

ADMISSION
Admission to all Washington-area Smithsonian museums, the National Zoo, and the National Museum of the American Indian, George Gustav Heye Center in New York is free. The Cooper Hewitt, Smithsonian Design Museum in New York charges admission.

Above: Edward Hopper (1882–1967), *Cape Cod Morning*, oil, 1950. Smithsonian American Art Museum. Below: "The Smithsonian Institution: America's Treasure Chest" offers a tantalizing sample of the breadth and depth of the Smithsonian's vast collections. Smithsonian Castle.

HOURS

Most Smithsonian museums are open daily, except December 25, from 10 A.M. to 5:30 P.M. (Check museum listings in this guide.) Extended summer hours are determined each year. The Anacostia Community Museum is open from 10 A.M. to 5 P.M. The Smithsonian American Art Museum and the National Portrait Gallery—located in the Donald W. Reynolds Center for American Art and Portraiture—are open from 11:30 A.M. to 7 P.M. The National Zoo hours: March–October: grounds are open from 8 A.M. to 7 P.M. and buildings from 10 A.M. to 6 P.M. (unless otherwise posted); November–February: grounds are open from 8 A.M. to 5 P.M. and buildings from 10 A.M. to 4:30 P.M. (unless otherwise posted).

HOW TO GET THERE

We recommend using public transportation, including taxis, when visiting Washington's attractions. Metrorail, Washington's subway system, and Metrobus link the downtown area with nearby communities in Maryland and Virginia. To locate the Metrorail station nearest the museum you wish to visit, see the individual

museum entries in this guide. For more information, call Metro at 202-637-7000 (voice/tape) or visit the Web site wmata.com.

The Smithsonian does not operate public parking facilities. Limited restricted street parking is available on and around the National Mall; posted times are enforced. Some commercial parking can be found in the area.

SMITHSONIAN VISITOR CENTER

Open daily (except December 25) from 8:30 A.M. to 5:30 P.M. in the Castle, the Smithsonian Visitor Center makes a great "gateway" for your journey—here you can find a new, interactive way to plan a route through exhibitions; get a grasp of the scope and scale of the Smithsonian; see collections highlights from each Smithsonian museum; watch a panda cam; tour the Castle and marvel at 19th-century architecture; find out what's going on around the Smithsonian; and consult with in-house experts about what to see and do. For general Smithsonian information, visit si.edu/contacts, call 202-633-1000 (voice/ tape), or write to Smithsonian Visitor Center, Smithsonian Institution, SI Building, Room 153, MRC 010, P.O. Box 37012, Washington, DC 20013-7012.

M. F. K. Fisher (1908–1992) by Ginny Stanford (b. 1950), acrylic on canvas, 1991. National Portrait Gallery. © Ginny Stanford.

ACCESSIBILITY

For information on access to the Smithsonian for visitors with disabilities, see the Web site at si.edu/visit/visitorswithdisabilites.

ONLINE INFORMATION

A wealth of information about the Smithsonian and its resources is available online at si.edu.

PHOTOGRAPHY

Video cameras are permitted for personal use in most museums. Photography is permitted in permanent-collection exhibitions but generally prohibited in special, temporary exhibitions. The use of flash attachments, monopods, tripods, and selfie sticks is prohibited in all buildings. Exceptions to these rules may occur in any exhibition or building. Ask at the information desk in the museum you are visiting for specific guidelines about photography.

Make the Smithsonian Visitor Center in the Castle your first stop. It opens at 8:30 A.M., earlier than the museums, so it's a great place to begin your visit. See previous page for details.

SERVICE ANIMALS

Service animals are permitted in all Smithsonian museums and the National Zoo. Pets are prohibited.

SMOKING

Smoking is prohibited in all Smithsonian facilities including the gardens.

WHERE TO EAT

Food service is available in the National Air and Space Museum on the National Mall and its Steven F. Udvar-Hazy Center in Chantilly, Virginia; the National Museum of African American History and Culture (opening in fall 2016); the National Museum of American History, Kenneth E. Behring Center; the National Museum of Natural History; the National Museum of the American Indian; and the Donald W. Reynolds Center for American Art and Portraiture. The Castle Café offers light fare daily. The Zoo has a variety of fast-food services.

MUSEUM STORES

Located in most Smithsonian museums, the stores
carry books, crafts, graphics, jewelry, reproductions,
toys, and gifts that relate to the museums' collections.

**The Chinese Moon Gate
in the Enid A. Haupt
Garden frames a view of
the Freer Gallery of Art.**

The National Mall has traditionally been the setting for large-scale events in the nation's capital.

THE NATIONAL MALL

A long, open, grassy stretch from the Capitol to the Washington Monument, the original National Mall was an important feature of Pierre L'Enfant's 1791 plan for the city of Washington. He envisioned it as a "vast esplanade" lined with grand residences. Before the Smithsonian Institution Building (the Castle) was built in the mid-19th century, however, the National Mall was used mainly for grazing and gardens. To the west, beyond the spot where the Washington Monument now stands, were tidal flats and marshes. After those areas were gradually filled, the National Mall was officially extended in the 20th century to the Lincoln Memorial.

In 1850, New York horticulturist Andrew Jackson Downing was commissioned to landscape the National

Mall. But his design, which called for curving carriage drives amid a grove of American evergreens, was only partly realized. By 1900, the National Mall had deteriorated. Its eyesores included a railroad station with sheds, tracks, and piles of coal. Two years later, work was begun to implement L'Enfant's early concept. Over the years, much of his vision has become reality, with the National Mall now lined by rows of great museum buildings.

On the National Mall today, people jog, fly kites, toss Frisbees, or just stroll. Near the Castle, children ride on an old-fashioned carousel. For a time each summer, the colorful Smithsonian Folklife Festival fills the National Mall with traditional music and crafts. On the benches alongside the walkways, visitors rest while deciding which Smithsonian museum to explore next.

THE STAR-SPANGLED BANNER

ABOUT THE

SMITHSONIAN

For many people, the red sandstone building that resembles a castle symbolizes the Smithsonian Institution. But the Smithsonian is much more than that. It encompasses 19 museums, the National Zoological Park, and numerous research facilities. Centered on the National Mall in Washington, DC, the Smithsonian has facilities in other parts of the nation's capital, a number of states, the Republic of Panama, Chile, and Belize.

The Smithsonian Institution is the world's largest museum complex and research center, with collections in every area of human interest numbering nearly 138 million items, ranging from a magnificent collection of ancient Chinese bronzes to the Hope diamond, from portraits of US presidents, to the Apollo lunar landing module, to a 3.5 billion-year-old fossil. The scope is staggering. All of these objects help us

understand the past, consider the present, and preserve history for future generations.

Only a small part of the Smithsonian's collections is on display in the museums at any one time, but we are putting more of our experts and objects online. On expeditions to all parts of the world, Smithsonian researchers continually gather new facts and make discoveries in the fields of art, science, history, and culture.

A CENTER FOR LEARNING

The Smithsonian is deeply involved in public education for people of all ages. Visiting groups of schoolchildren are common sights in the museums, and families come together here on weekend outings and summer vacations. Educators from the elementary school through the university level use the Smithsonian's resources, as do scholars pursuing advanced research. Through public classes, lectures, performances, and studio arts courses, the Smithsonian Associates offers a wide range of lifelong learning opportunities.

The Smithsonian also offers an exciting schedule of "living exhibits." Performing-arts activities include music, theater, dance, film programs, and Discovery Theater performances for youngsters. The Smithsonian Latino Center (latino.si.edu) develops and supports curatorial positions, research, exhibitions, public and educational programs, Web content, and collections that highlight and advance Latino contribution in art, science, culture, and the humanities.

The Smithsonian Asian Pacific American Center is an innovative museum lab for understanding the Asian Pacific American experience. The Smithsonian Science Education Center (ssec.si.edu), an organization of the Smithsonian and the National Academies, works to improve the learning and teaching of science for all students in the United States and throughout the world.

Preceding pages: After a two-year renovation, the National Museum of American History reopened to the public in 2008 with a Grand Reopening Festival. Historical characters, including George Washington, mingle with the public.

Opposite: Willem de Kooning (1904–1997), *Woman, Sag Harbor*, 1964, oil and charcoal on wood. Hirshhorn Museum and Sculpture Garden.

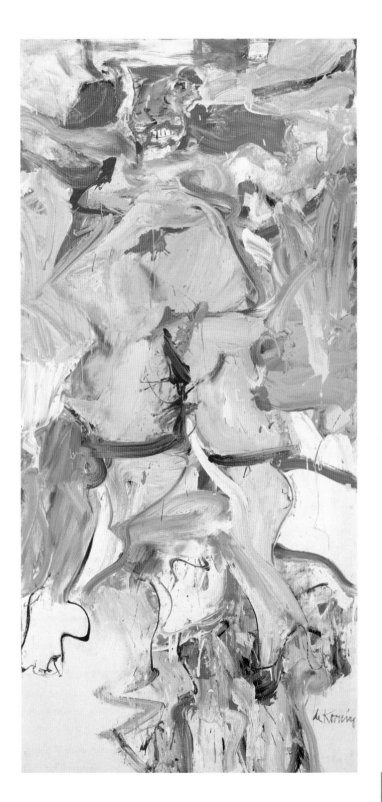

Clockwise from top: Conard and Jones Co., *1916 Floral Guide*, 1916; Owen Jones, *Examples of Chinese Ornament: Selected from Objects in the South Kensington Museum and Other Collections*, 1867; John F. C. Mullen, *Official Guide of the Centennial Exposition of the Ohio Valley and Central States: Cincinnati, O., U.S.A. 1888*. Smithsonian Libraries

SMITHSONIAN FOLKLIFE FESTIVAL

Every summer on the National Mall, the Smithsonian Folklife Festival celebrates traditional and folk cultures of the nation and beyond. By inviting artisans, musicians, cooks, dancers, and other experts to share their stories, songs, and experiences— and encouraging visitors to join in—the Festival offers a vibrant stage for sustaining traditions and promoting cross-cultural engagement.

SMITHSONIAN LIBRARIES

This 21-branch library system boasts collections of two million volumes, in science, history, art, and technology, including more than 40,000 rare books and 10,000 exceptional manuscripts. Smithsonian Libraries holdings also include a unique and distinguished collection of manufacturers' trade literature (480,000 pieces representing 35,000 companies) and World's Fair materials. All libraries may be visited by appointment. Digital exhibitions and digitized editions of rare books are on view online at library.si.edu. (For information about the Smithsonian Libraries Exhibition Gallery, see the entry on the National Museum of American History, Kenneth E. Behring Center in this guide.)

NATIONAL OUTREACH

As a national institution, the Smithsonian takes cultural and educational programs to people across the country. The Smithsonian Associates develops and presents programming designed for audiences of all

ages primarily in the Washington, DC, area but also for communities and classrooms nationally. Smithsonian Affiliations is a unique outreach program that shares Smithsonian collections, staff experts, researchers, and educational resources with communities across the country. The Smithsonian Center for Learning and Digital Access offers educational resources to teachers

Through educationally focused museum sleepovers, summer camps, and performances at Discovery Theater, the Smithsonian Associates serves children and their families.

and students and endeavors to make the Smithsonian a learning laboratory for everyone. The Smithsonian Institution Traveling Exhibition Service shares the wealth of Smithsonian collections and research with millions of people outside Washington, DC, through exhibitions about art, science, and history. (For more information on these national programs, see "Smithsonian Across America" at the back of this guide.) Smithsonian publications make available the expertise that its scholars assemble. *Smithsonian* and *Air & Space/Smithsonian* magazines publish lively articles on topics inspired by Smithsonian activities. Through the World Wide Web, home and school computer users have instant access to a rich resource with which to plan a visit, conduct research, find out about programs and exhibitions, and communicate with the Smithsonian.

RESEARCH AT THE SMITHSONIAN

The Smithsonian is a preeminent research center. Its research activities are known throughout the world for their benefit to the scholarly community and the advancement of knowledge. Smithsonian scientists, historians, and art historians explore topics as diverse as global environmental concerns, the nature of the world's changing human and social systems, and the care and preservation of museum objects.

ARCHIVES OF AMERICAN ART

The Archives collects and preserves materials and makes available primary sources documenting the history of the visual arts in the United States. Headquartered in Washington, DC, the Archives also has a research center in New York City. For information, call 202-633-7940.

MUSEUM CONSERVATION INSTITUTE

The Museum Conservation Institute (MCI) is the center for specialized technical collections research and conservation for all Smithsonian museums and collections. MCI staff collaborates with and serves as a resource for in-depth studies of art, anthropological and historical objects, and natural history and biological materials using the most advanced analytical techniques to elucidate their provenance, composition, and cultural context. MCI studies are also used to improve the Smithsonian's conservation and collections storage capabilities. Such studies require the latest instrumentation, analytical expertise, and knowledge of archaeology, art history, biology, chemistry, conservation,

conservation science, geology, mechanical engineering, and interpretive abilities, all of which are available through MCI. For more information, call 301-238-1240 or visit MCI's Web site at si.edu/mci.

A Smithsonian Environmental Research Center technician measures the effects of exposure to increased concentrations of atmospheric carbon dioxide on accumulation of soil carbon in a brackish tidal marsh.

SMITHSONIAN CONSERVATION BIOLOGY INSTITUTE

The Smithsonian Conservation Biology Institute, which launched on January 25, 2010, serves as an umbrella for the Smithsonian's global effort to conserve species and train future generations of conservationists. The SCBI is headquartered in Front Royal, Virginia, at the facility previously known as the National Zoo's Conservation and Research Center..

SMITHSONIAN MARINE STATION AT FORT PIERCE

This research facility of the National Museum of Natural History serves as a field station that draws more than 100 top scientists and students each year. Research focuses on the marine biodiversity and ecosystems of the Indian River Lagoon and the nearshore waters of Florida's east central coast. The station has also teamed with community partners to create a marine science outreach center and public aquarium. For information, visit sms.si.edu.

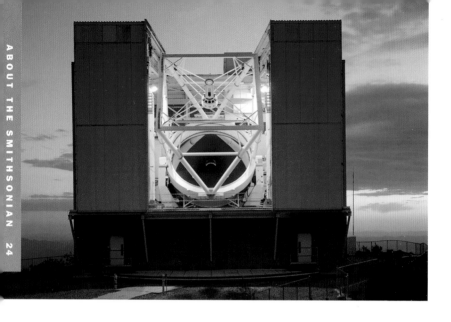

The Smithsonian
Astrophysical
Observatory's MMT
Telescope glows against
the Arizona sunset.

SMITHSONIAN ASTROPHYSICAL OBSERVATORY

This research center is part of the Harvard-Smithsonian Center for Astrophysics (SAO) in Cambridge, Massachusetts. Smithsonian scientists are recognized leaders in theoretical astrophysics, ground-based gamma-ray astronomy, solar and stellar physics, extrasolar planets, the Milky Way and other galaxies, and the dynamics and evolution of the Universe. SAO has observatories in Arizona, Hawaii, Chile, and Antarctica. The largest field facility is the Fred Lawrence Whipple Observatory on Mount Hopkins near Tucson, Arizona. SAO also manages the control center for NASA's Chandra X-Ray Observatory. For information regarding public programs, visit cfa.harvard.edu or call the Public Affairs Office in Cambridge at 617-495-7461 or the Whipple Observatory at 520-879-4407.

SMITHSONIAN ENVIRONMENTAL RESEARCH CENTER

The Smithsonian Environmental Research Center (SERC) provides science-based knowledge to meet critical environmental challenges. SERC leads objective research on coastal ecosystems—where land meets the sea—to inform real-world decisions for wise policies, best business practices, and a sustainable planet. SERC's headquarters in Edgewater, Maryland, comprise

2,650 acres of diverse landscape and 16 miles of protected shoreline on the nation's largest estuary—Chesapeake Bay—25 miles east of Washington, DC. The site serves as a natural laboratory for long-term and cutting-edge ecological research. Here the Smithsonian explores the earth's most pressing environmental issues, including toxic chemicals, water quality, invasive species, land use, depleted fisheries, and global change. SERC also explains environmental science in innovative ways that transform how people view the biosphere and inspire them to take active roles in sustainable stewardship of the planet. SERC leads networks of research and education that extend across the coasts of the United States and around the world. For information, call 443-482-2200 or visit serc.si.edu.

SMITHSONIAN TROPICAL RESEARCH INSTITUTE

Headquartered in the Republic of Panama, the Smithsonian Tropical Research Institute is the world's premier tropical biology research organization, dedicated to increasing understanding of the past, present and future of tropical biodiversity and its relevance to human welfare.

STRI's basic research is conducted primarily in tropical forest and coral reef ecosystems. STRI scientists discover new organisms, test scientific explanations for ecological adaptation and evolutionary innovation, develop methods to restore degraded lands, train students, and promote conservation of tropical ecosystems.

STRI also coordinates the Center for Tropical Forest Science–Smithsonian Institution Global Earth Observatory (CTFS–ForestGEO), a global network of more than 60 forest research and monitoring stations on five continents. For information, visit stri.org.

Democracy dilemma: Sabrina Amador, post-doctoral fellow at the Smithsonian in Panama, asks how acacia ants "decide" who will do a given task. Social insect behavior provides clues about the organization of more complex societies.

HISTORY OF THE SMITHSONIAN

The Smithsonian owes its origin to James Smithson, a British scientist who never visited the United States. Smithson named his nephew Henry James Hungerford as the beneficiary in his will. He stipulated that should Hungerford die without heirs (as he did in 1835), the entire Smithson fortune bequeathed to Hungerford would go to this country. The purpose would be to "found at Washington, under the name of the Smithsonian Institution, an establishment for the increase and diffusion of knowledge."

On July 1, 1836, Congress accepted Smithson's legacy and pledged the faith of the United States to the charitable trust. In 1838, after British courts had approved the bequest, the nation received Smithson's estate—bags of gold sovereigns, then the equivalent of more than a half-million dollars, a great fortune in those days. Eight years later, on August 10, 1846, President James K. Polk signed an act of Congress establishing the Smithsonian Institution in its present form and providing for the administration of the Smithson trust, independent of the government, by a Board of Regents and Secretary of the Smithsonian. With the formal creation of the Smithsonian came a commitment to the work that continues today in research, the operation of museums and libraries, and the dissemination of information in the fields of science, art, and history.

Today, the Smithsonian is a national institution that receives a substantial appropriation from the federal government. Essential funding also comes from private sources, including the Smithson trust, other endowments, individuals, foundations, corporations, and revenues raised from such activities as membership programs, a mail-order catalog, museum stores, and food services.

The chief executive officer of the Smithsonian is the Secretary. The Institution is governed by a Board of Regents, which by law is composed of the vice president of the United States, the chief justice of the United States, three members of the Senate,

A statue of Joseph Henry, first Secretary of the Smithsonian, enjoys a prominent setting at the Castle's entrance on the National Mall.

three members of the House of Representatives, and
nine private citizens. The chief justice has traditionally
served as chancellor of the Smithsonian.

Each museum has its own director and staff.
The central administration of the Smithsonian is
headquartered in the Castle building.

THE CASTLE

The Smithsonian Institution Building, popularly known
as the Castle, was designed in medieval revival style (a
19th-century combination of late Romanesque and
early Gothic motifs) by James Renwick Jr., architect of
Grace Church and St. Patrick's Cathedral in New York
and the Renwick Gallery of the Smithsonian American
Art Museum in Washington.

A disastrous fire in 1865—just ten years after the
Castle was completed—caused extensive damage and
the loss of valuable objects. Restoration of the building
took two years. In the 1880s, the Castle was enlarged
and much of it remodeled.

The Castle originally housed the entire Smithsonian,
which included a science museum, a lecture hall, an art
gallery, research laboratories, administrative offices,
and living quarters for the Secretary and his family.

The Smithsonian
Institution Building,
known as the Castle,
was designed by
architect James
Renwick Jr. and
completed in 1855.

Today, administrative offices, the Smithsonian Visitor Center, and an exhibition titled "The Smithsonian Institution: America's Treasure Chest" are located here. The Smithsonian Visitor Center opens daily (except December 25) at 8:30 A.M. Here, visitors can get questions answered by volunteer information specialists and pick up free brochures on the Smithsonian.

SMITHSONIAN GARDENS

Smithsonian Gardens has created several beautiful spaces around the Smithsonian museums on the National Mall. All have been designed to complement the museums they border and enhance the overall museum experience. Staff and docents lead weekly tours of some of the gardens from May through September (weather permitting). Visit any information desk for details.

The Enid A. Haupt Garden (left) is enlivened with a cascade of water in the Fountain Garden that provides a cool respite during the summer months. A historic cast-iron fountain (above) adorns the center of the Kathrine Dulin Folger Rose Garden. From mid-May through November, roses grace the garden with color and fragrance. Bulbs, perennials, annuals, tropical plants, and evergreens enhance the garden's year-round beauty.

The south side of the Mall features the Enid A. Haupt Garden, a 4.2 acre garden named for its philanthropic donor. An ornate parterre in the center is flanked by the Asian-inspired Moon Gate and the Moorish Fountain Garden. Other gardens on this side of the Mall include the Freer Gallery of Art's formal courtyard garden; the fragrant Kathrine Dulin Folger Rose Garden next to the Smithsonian Castle; the colorful Mary Livingston Ripley Garden; and the Hirshhorn Museum and Sculpture Garden, where the plantings provide an ever-changing backdrop for the large-scale artworks on display outdoors. The native landscape at the National Museum of the American Indian and terraced beds at the National Air and Space Museum provide year-round interest for visitors.

On the Mall's north side, extensive landscape design at the National Museum of African American History and Culture includes a green roof, reading grove, water feature, pavilion with seating, and oculus, which brings light into the museum's Contemplative Court. The Victory Garden at the National Museum of American History is typical of vegetable gardens planted during World War II, while the nearby Heirloom Garden

The Enid A. Haupt Garden (above) sits atop an underground complex of museums and is therefore a rooftop garden. It comprises three separate garden spaces, each reflecting the cultural influences celebrated in the adjacent architecture and museums. Nestled between the Arts and Industries Building and the Hirshhorn Museum and Sculpture Garden, the Mary Livingston Ripley Garden (right) displays dozens of unusual varieties of plants in raised beds along a curvilinear brick path.

showcases favorites cultivated in American gardens before 1950. The Pollinator Garden and the Urban Bird Habitat at the National Museum of Natural History spotlight plantings that provide food and shelter for migrating wildlife species.

Beneath the Haupt Garden is a three-level underground museum, research, and education complex that contains the Arthur M. Sackler Gallery, the National Museum of African Art, and the S. Dillon Ripley Center. The museums are accessible through aboveground entrance pavilions. Through a bronze-domed kiosk, visitors enter the Ripley Center, named for the Smithsonian's eighth Secretary. It currently houses the International Gallery with its changing exhibitions, workshops and classrooms for public programs, and a lecture hall. The Smithsonian Associates and the Contributing Membership Program have their offices in the Ripley Center.

SMITHSONIAN SECRETARIES: 1846 TO TODAY*

JOSEPH HENRY [1846–78], a physical scientist and pioneer and inventor in electricity, was founding Secretary. Henry set the Smithsonian's course with an emphasis on science.

Naturalist SPENCER FULLERTON BAIRD [1878–87] developed the early Smithsonian museums and promoted the accumulation of natural history specimens and collections of all kinds.

SAMUEL PIERPONT LANGLEY [1887–1906], whose focus was aeronautics, astrophysics, and astronomy, launched the Smithsonian in those directions. During the administration of CHARLES DOOLITTLE WALCOTT [1907–27], a geologist and paleontologist, the National Museum of Natural History and the Freer Gallery of Art opened, and the National Collection of Fine Arts (now Smithsonian American Art Museum) became a separate museum.

CHARLES GREELEY ABBOT [1928–44], a specialist in solar radiation and solar power, established a bureau to study the effect of light on plant and animal life—the precursor of the Smithsonian Environmental Research Center. During the tenure of ornithologist ALEXANDER WETMORE [1945–52], the National Air Museum (now National Air and Space Museum) and the Canal Biological Area (now Smithsonian Tropical Research Institute) became part of the Institution.

LEONARD CARMICHAEL [1953–64], a physiological psychologist and former president of Tufts University, oversaw the opening of the National Museum of History and Technology (now National Museum of American History, Behring Center).

Under the leadership of S. DILLON RIPLEY [1964–84], a biologist, ecologist, and authority on birds of East Asia, the Smithsonian added the Hirshhorn Museum and Sculpture Garden, the National Museum of African Art, the Renwick Gallery, and the Cooper-Hewitt, National Design Museum (now Cooper Hewitt, Smithsonian Design Museum). The National Air and Space Museum moved to its building on the Mall, and construction began on the underground complex for the National Museum of African Art and the Arthur M. Sackler Gallery. Ripley also encouraged innovative ways of serving a wider public.

ROBERT Mc.C. ADAMS [1984–94], an anthropologist, archaeologist, and former university administrator, placed new emphasis on broadening the involvement of diverse cultural communities and enhancing research support and educational outreach. The National Museum of the American Indian was established as part of the Smithsonian during his administration.

I. MICHAEL HEYMAN [1994–99], a law professor and former chancellor of the University of California at Berkeley, guided the Smithsonian to reach out to Americans who do not visit Washington, DC. Initiatives included the first traveling exhibition of Smithsonian treasures, for the Institution's 150th anniversary; a Smithsonian Web site; and the Affiliations Program for the long-term loan of collections.

During the tenure of LAWRENCE M. SMALL [2000–2007], the Smithsonian opened the National Air and Space Museum's Steven F. Udvar-Hazy Center and the National Museum of the American Indian; reopened the newly renovated/named Donald W. Reynolds Center for American Art and Portraiture; and established the National Museum of African American History and Culture.

G. WAYNE CLOUGH [2008–14] expanded the Smithsonian's global relevance and helped shape the nation's future through emphasis on research, education, and scientific discovery. He initiated long-range planning for the Institution; made more of the collections accessible through a digitization effort; and oversaw the opening of Sant Ocean Hall at the National Museum of Natural History and the reopening of the National Museum of American History.

DR. DAVID J. SKORTON assumed his position as the 13th secretary in 2015. As a board-certified cardiologist, he is the first physician to lead the Smithsonian. An ardent and nationally recognized supporter of the arts and humanities, Skorton has called for a national dialogue to emphasize the importance of funding for these disciplines. He asserts that supporting the arts and humanities is a wise investment in the future of the country. *Dates in brackets signify years as Secretary

ESPECIALLY FOR CHILDREN

THINGS TO SEE AND DO AT THE SMITHSONIAN

Before your visit, print a copy of "Tips for Visiting Smithsonian Museums with Children" at si.edu/visit/kids or call Smithsonian Information at 202-633-1000 (voice/tape) to request a copy.

NATIONAL AIR AND SPACE MUSEUM

Both locations of the National Air and Space Museum (on the National Mall and in Chantilly, Virginia) offer a range of programs for families, children, and school groups. Stories, hands-on activities, science demonstrations, interactive displays, and special family-oriented days are offered. Check at the museums' Welcome Centers for a calendar of events and ask about activites scheduled for the day. Older children especially enjoy the flight simulator rides and spectacular films shown on the five-story-high screens in the IMAX® Theaters. At the National Mall building, multimedia programs on astronomy and space in the Albert Einstein Planetarium are always popular. Simulators and shows have fees.

NATIONAL MUSEUM OF NATURAL HISTORY

Even after a tour of the museum's best-known treasures, families and children have much, much more to do here.

• Hundreds of live butterflies flit from flower to flower, sip nectar, and roost inside the cocoon-like butterfly pavilion in *Butterflies + Plants: Partners in Evolution*. To purchase a ticket, visit butterflies.si. edu, call 1-866-868-7774 or visit the pavilion box office.

• Next door at the Insect Zoo, children crawl through a termite mound, examine a real beehive, and hold insects. Staff members feed the tarantulas several times a day as an excited audience looks on.

• Q?rius (pronounced *curious*), The Coralyn W. Whitney Science Education Center, combines the properties of scientific labs, collections vaults, creative studios, and hangout spots to encourage teen and tween visitors, their families, and their teachers to explore the world with curiosity and excitement. Q?rius jr.—A Discovery Room helps the youngest visitors get excited about science. Touchable objects, kid-focused displays, and enthusiastic helpers encourage them to experiment, observe, and ask questions about what they see. Children must be accompanied by an adult.

• In the Samuel C. Johnson IMAX® Theater, visitors might take a fantastic journey through time or visit an exotic location in the 400-seat theater, which shows 2-D and 3-D films on its six-story screen. Tickets are available at the IMAX® box office for a fee. Visit si.edu/imax or call 1-866-868-7774 for more information.

NATIONAL MUSEUM OF AMERICAN HISTORY,
KENNETH E. BEHRING CENTER

Young visitors can charge their imaginations at the Spark!Lab; see the enchanting 23-room dollhouse; climb aboard a Chicago Transit Authority car in "America on the Move"; and more.

SPARK!LAB

Everybody can envision the "Eureka!" moment of invention, when the idea suddenly strikes and—BOOM—a new product is ready to change the world.

Spark!Lab is a hands-on space for visitors of all ages that features games, science experiments, and inventors' notebooks, with a special section for kids under age 5.

PATRICK F. TAYLOR FOUNDATION "OBJECT PROJECT"

"Object Project" presents familiar objects in a new light, exploring how people, innovations, and social change shaped life as we know it. Visitors have the opportunity to see and handle objects—from refrigerators and bicycles to ready-to-wear clothing and household conveniences as diverse as window screens and deodorant—and explore their significance through historic documents and compelling activities. Encompassing almost 4,000 square feet, this display features some 300 objects, a

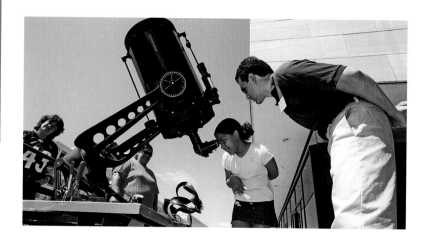

"magic" scrapbook, and a special version of "The Price Is Right," and offers visitors the chance to try on clothing virtually.

WEGMANS WONDERPLACE

This space allows curious kids ages 5 and under to "cook" in a kitchen inspired by Julia Child's; plant and harvest pretend vegetables and run the farm stand; find the owls hiding in a miniature replica of the Smithsonian's Castle building; and captain a tugboat based on a model in the museum's collection. Here we nurture the motivation behind innovation—the sense of wonder that causes us to ask why . . . or why not.

Please inquire about special activities and exhibitions, ask at the Welcome Center on the second floor or the information desk on the first floor, call 202-633-1000 (voice/tape), or visit the museum's Web site at americanhistory.si.edu.

FREER GALLERY OF ART AND ARTHUR M. SACKLER GALLERY

The popular ImaginAsia program, which includes inspirational art tours and workshops for making hands-on projects to take home, offers young visitors the chance to discover Asian art and culture. The museum also frequently hosts family festivals celebrating different cultural areas and provides activity guides. For more information and a full schedule, visit asia.si.edu.

NATIONAL MUSEUM OF AFRICAN ART

The arts and cultures of Africa are introduced to young audiences through workshops, storytelling, musical performances, and other activities. The popular "Let's Read About Africa" program, for children ages 5–10, introduces young audiences to current and classical children's literature about Africa. Programs for families are offered with many special exhibitions.

HIRSHHORN MUSEUM AND SCULPTURE GARDEN

ARTLAB+ is a digital-media studio that provides teens with free after-school drop-in programs and gives them a safe space in which to learn and explore. Teens work with artist mentors to create

works using audio engineering, video production, digital photography, graphic illustration, game design, 3-D design, sculpture, and creative writing. Programming encourages participants to become critical thinkers and hone their technological skills. The curriculum is driven by the interests of the teens, who are given the freedom to direct their own learning experiences.

NATIONAL PORTRAIT GALLERY

Programs for children and their families at the National Portrait Gallery offer innovative experiences for young visitors in the galleries and its Education Center, located on the first floor of the museum. For more information about upcoming programs, visit the gallery's Web site at npg.si.edu or call 202-633-8501.

SMITHSONIAN AMERICAN ART MUSEUM

Kids of all ages will delight in finding artworks made from bottle caps, tin foil, or televisions throughout the museum. Hands-on "Art á la Cart" mobile gallery stations engage family visitors with interactive experiences. Other free programs include Family Festivals, artist demonstrations, and musical performances. Developing scientists can watch conservators treat art treasures in the Lunder Conservation Center, and future curators can browse more than 3,000 objects in the Luce Foundation Center for American Art. Look for upcoming programs on the museum's Web site at americanart.si.edu.

In addition, the Luce Foundation Center offers weekly tours, a daily self-guided scavenger hunt, and an informal sketching program. ASL and verbal description tours for deaf and visually impaired visitors are available twice monthly, or by prior arrangement. Check the museum's Web site for details.

The museum offers a variety of online activities, including *Picturing the 1930s,* a virtual 3-D movie theater; *Meet Me at Midnight,* an interactive online adventure; and *¡del Corazón!,* which features interviews with Latino artists. Look for the fun at americanart.si.edu/ education/activities/online.

RENWICK GALLERY OF THE SMITHSONIAN AMERICAN ART MUSEUM

The Renwick Gallery offers a number of public programs and Family Festivals for children of all ages. Activities range from craft demonstrations and gallery talks to hands-on workshops with artists and musical performances. Look for upcoming programs on the museum's Web site at americanart.si.edu.

NATIONAL POSTAL MUSEUM

With state-of-the-art interactive displays, inviting exhibit design, and activities geared to adults and children, the museum is designed for a family audience. Spend time in some of the museum's many audiovisual and interactive areas, including computer kiosks where you can personalize souvenir postcards. Climb aboard a big-

rig cab, a mud wagon, and a railway mail car. Discover the story of Owney, a stray dog who became the mascot for the Railway Mail Service. Check the museum's Web site for the current schedule of public programs and participate in a variety of hands-on activities and crafts.

ANACOSTIA COMMUNITY MUSEUM

Anacostia Community Museum features year-round school tours, teacher trainings, a Youth Advisory Council, career days, annual family festivals, an after-

school and summer program for elementary students and a model environmental project for secondary school youth and teachers. Also available are numerous volunteer opportunities including internships for high school as well as ongoing youth-centered public programs that involve storytelling, art workshops, performances and films.

NATIONAL ZOO

Giant pandas, big cats, elephants, great apes, and reptiles are Zoo favorites for children of all ages. To see the pandas when they are most active, visit early in the day. Observe elephants being trained on the Elephant Trails or outside (weather permitting), or watch seals and sea lions being fed and trained.

In the Amazonia rain forest exhibition, explore "Amphibian Alert" to see endangered frogs, salamanders, and caecilians. The Reptile Discovery Center features hands-on activities and the chance to see an endangered Komodo dragon, the world's largest lizard.

Daily programs include animal training and enrichment, feeding, and talks by keepers. Demonstrations are good opportunities for visitors to discover more about the animals from the people who care for them every day. Check the Daily Programs schedule on the Zoo's Web site at nationalzoo.si.edu.

NATIONAL MUSEUM OF THE AMERICAN INDIAN

The National Museum of the American Indian (NMAI), in Washington, DC, offers a variety of engaging opportunities for families that will expand their knowledge of and appreciation for Native cultures and traditions throughout the Americas. Families can enjoy their visits to the museum by obtaining free Family Guides at the Welcome Desk, participating in hands-on activities, attending regularly scheduled Family Days, taking a family or landscape tour, or seeing a film.

Throughout the year the museum offers a wide variety of craft demonstrations and performances that feature Native cultural arts—music, dance, drama, literature, and storytelling—in indoor and outdoor program venues. Be sure to stop by the Welcome Desk to learn which programs will be available on the day of your visit.

The NMAI's George Gustav Heye Center in New York City hosts Native musicians, dancers, artists, and elders in presentations of their art and cultural heritage in informal programs that enable families to learn firsthand about the lifeways and world views of Native peoples. Kids can enjoy such diverse programs as theatrical presentations, hands-on workshops, storytelling programs, and annual events such as the Children's Festival and the Native Sounds Downtown concert series.

COOPER HEWITT, SMITHSONIAN DESIGN MUSEUM

The collections of the museum as well as design basics are introduced to young visitors through various family programs including "Design Tales" for preschoolers and "Imagination Playground" where children engage in visualization and creative play. The museum also hosts "Design Camp" every summer for ages 7—12; at camp, visitors take part in fun challenges, gallery explorations, and experience the design process through sketching, building, and playing.

CAROUSEL ON THE MALL

For a perfect break from museums for adults and children, take a ride on the carousel on the National Mall near the Smithsonian Castle. The carousel operates daily (weather permitting) on a seasonal schedule and charges a small fee.

DISCOVERY THEATER

Located in the S. Dillon Ripley Center, this popular theater for young audiences approximately ages 2–16 presents live performances by storytellers, puppeteers, dancers, actors, and singers year-round. For show times, tickets, performance location, and reservations, call 202-633-8700 Monday through Friday, or visit discoverytheater.org.

Above: The Bell X-1 *Glamorous Glennis* cockpit remains much the same as it was when Chuck Yeager first exceeded the speed of sound on October 14, 1947. Opposite top: Boeing F4B-40. Opposite bottom: *Continuum*, a cast-bronze sculpture by Charles O. Perry, installed in front of the museum's Independence Avenue entrance.

NATIONAL AIR AND SPACE MUSEUM

In Washington, DC
Independence Avenue
at 6th Street, SW.
Mall entrance:
Jefferson Drive at
6th Street, SW.
Open daily from
10 A.M. to 5:30 P.M.
Closed December 25.
Metrorail: L'Enfant
Plaza station.
Information:
202-633-2214

In Chantilly, VA
Steven F. Udvar-Hazy
Center, 14390 Air
and Space Museum
Pkwy., off Rte. 28.
Open daily from
10 A.M. to 5:30 P.M.
Closed December 25.
Parking available for
a fee. Information:
703-572-4118
TTY: 202-357-1729
(both locations)
airandspace.si.edu

When visitors come to Washington, DC, it's almost a sure bet that the National Air and Space Museum is the first place they'll go. People of all ages and backgrounds are drawn by its reputation as one of the world's most visited museums. Once inside, their high expectations are surpassed as they wander among icons of aviation and space and enjoy activities such as large-screen IMAX® movies, flight simulators, planetarium shows, guided tours, science demonstrations, and interactive devices.

The museum has two public display facilities. The museum in Washington, DC, showcases many one-of-a-kind artifacts, including the original 1903 Wright Flyer, Charles Lindbergh's *Spirit of St. Louis,* Amelia Earhart's Lockheed Vega, John Glenn's *Friendship 7* spacecraft, and the

Below: The museum's Viking Lander is a test vehicle like the two that soft-landed on Mars in 1976 and sent back images and data from the surface. Opposite: The Bell X-1 *Glamorous Glennis*, the first airplane to fly faster than the speed of sound, hangs in the Boeing Milestones of Flight Hall in the Smithsonian's National Air and Space Museum.

Apollo 11 command module. The Steven F. Udvar-Hazy Center in Chantilly, Virginia, exhibits thousands of artifacts—including a Lockheed SR-71 Blackbird, a Concorde, the Boeing B-29 Superfortress *Enola Gay,* and the space shuttle *Discovery*—in an open, hangar-like setting.

Within these two remarkable facilities—which comprise the largest complex in the world for presenting the history of air and space—visitors can marvel at the National Air and Space Museum's enormous, globally renowned collection.

THE MUSEUM IN WASHINGTON, DC

The museum in Washington, DC, presents the story of aeronautics and space flight in 23 galleries, each devoted to a specific subject or theme. Hundreds of historically significant aircraft, rockets, spacecraft, engines, scale models, pilot uniforms, spacesuits, awards, artworks, instruments, and pieces of flight equipment are on display.

A good place to start is just inside the entrances at either side of the building, where you are surrounded by some of the most important airplanes, rockets, and spacecraft in history.

GALLERY 100. Milestones of Flight
The central gallery of the museum—in more ways than one.

GROUND LEVEL

MERCURY *FRIENDSHIP 7.* Spacecraft employed in the first US piloted orbital flight, flown by astronaut John Glenn, 1962.

GEMINI IV. Spacecraft used in the first US spacewalk, 1965.

TOUCHABLE MOON ROCK. Collected from the lunar surface by Apollo 17 astronauts

STAR TREK STARSHIP ENTERPRISE STUDIO MODEL. Used in filming the 1960s TV show.

LUNAR MODULE (LM2). Intended for flight but used instead for tests on Earth before the Moon landing, the LM2 display is a highly accurate depiction of the Apollo 11 Lunar Module *Eagle* (LM5) on the Moon.

The Ryan NYP *Spirit of St. Louis* in which Charles Lindbergh made his historic solo nonstop transatlantic flight from New York to Paris.

MAY 1926 GODDARD ROCKET. The world's oldest surviving liquid-fuel rocket

THE RUTAN *VOYAGER*. In 1986, *Voyager* became the first aircraft to fly around the world nonstop without refueling.

NASA FULL-SCALE WIND TUNNEL FAN. Built in 1931 for the National Advisory Committee for Aeronautics (NACA), predecessor to the National Air and Space Administration (NASA), the wind tunnel was used to test most of America's significant military aircraft of its era.

VIKING LANDER. Test vehicle for the first spacecraft to operate on the surface of Mars, 1976

PERSHING-II (US) AND SS-20 (USSR) MISSILES. Two disarmed missiles that represent the more than 2,600 nuclear intermediate-range ballistic missiles banned by the Intermediate Nuclear Forces Treaty of 1987

THE SPACE MURAL: A COSMIC VIEW. Robert T. McCall's conception of the creation of the Universe, the triumph of lunar exploration, and an optimistic look at the future

EARTH FLIGHT ENVIRONMENT. Eric Sloane's dramatic depiction of the remarkable ocean of air that is our atmosphere

SUSPENDED FROM THE CEILING

SPACESHIP ONE. First privately developed piloted vehicle to reach space, 2004

BELL X-1 *GLAMOROUS GLENNIS*. First airplane to fly faster than the speed of sound, piloted by Charles E. "Chuck" Yeager, 1947

RYAN NYP *SPIRIT OF ST. LOUIS*. Airplane in which Charles Lindbergh made the first solo nonstop transatlantic flight, 1927

BELL XP-59A AIRACOMET. First American turbojet aircraft, 1942

EXPLORER 1. Backup for the first US satellite to orbit Earth, 1958

SPUTNIK 1. Soviet replica of the first artificial satellite to orbit Earth, 1957

PIONEER 10. Prototype for the first unmanned spacecraft to fly by Jupiter and Saturn and out of the solar system, launched in 1972

NORTH AMERICAN X-15. First piloted aircraft to exceed six times the speed of sound

and the first to explore the fringes of space, 1967

MARINER 2. Backup of the first interplanetary probe to study another planet (Venus), 1962

SpaceShipOne, the first privately built and piloted vehicle to reach space, is on display in the National Air and Space Museum in Washington, DC

The most successful airliner in history, the Douglas DC-3 dominated both commercial and military air transportation from its introduction in 1935 until after World War II. It was the first airplane that could make money by carrying only passengers. This one flew nearly 57,000 hours for Eastern Air Lines from 1937 to 1952.

GALLERY 101. Museum Store

PITTS S-15 SPECIAL. Small aerobatic biplane designed by Curtis Pitts. It dominated the unlimited class in world-championship competition, 1960

GALLERY 102. America by Air

The story of America's airline industry

DOUGLAS DC-3. A design milestone and perhaps the single most important aircraft in air transportation history, 1935. At 16,875 pounds, the heaviest airplane hanging from the museum's ceiling

FORD 5-AT TRI-MOTOR. Offered dependable, safe, and relatively comfortable service when introduced in 1928

PITCAIRN PA-5 MAILWING. Efficient, reliable airmail carrier, first flown in 1927

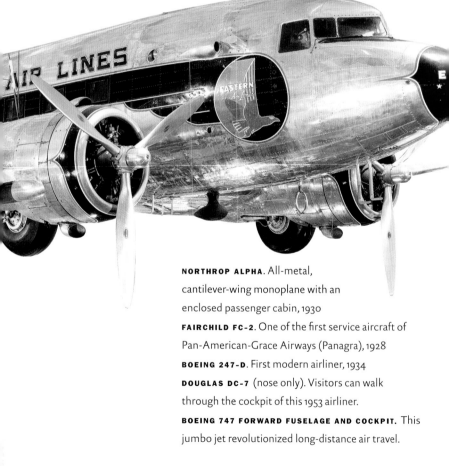

NORTHROP ALPHA. All-metal, cantilever-wing monoplane with an enclosed passenger cabin, 1930

FAIRCHILD FC-2. One of the first service aircraft of Pan-American-Grace Airways (Panagra), 1928

BOEING 247-D. First modern airliner, 1934

DOUGLAS DC-7 (nose only). Visitors can walk through the cockpit of this 1953 airliner.

BOEING 747 FORWARD FUSELAGE AND COCKPIT. This jumbo jet revolutionized long-distance air travel.

GALLERY 103.

Choose from a variety of ride simulations, including an excursion to the International Space Station and a sortie in various vintage aircraft. Or climb aboard one of ten interactive flight simulators and try to become a jet combat "ace" as you pilot the simulator into 360-degree barrel rolls. Choose either pilot or gunner responsibilities.

GALLERY 104. Military Unmanned Aerial Vehicles (UAVs)

Unmanned vehicles for reconnaissance purposes and versions armed with weapons, ranging from the large and lethal to the tiny and portable

GENERAL ATOMICS AERONAUTICAL SYSTEMS, INC. MQ-1L PREDATOR A. Predators have performed missions over the Balkans, Afghanistan, and Iraq. The one hanging here flew 196 combat missions in Afghanistan.

BOEING X-45A JOINT UNMANNED COMBAT AIR SYSTEM (J-UCAS). Stealthy, swept-wing, and jet-powered, the first modern UAV designed specifically for combat strike missions

AEROVIRONMENT RQ-14A DRAGON EYE. By far the smallest aircraft here, this hand- or bungee-launched mini-UAV can provide reconnaissance and surveillance information to field commanders.

PIONEER UAV RQ-2A PIONEER. The RQ-2A provides field commanders with real-time reconnaissance, surveillance, target acquisition, and battle damage information.

The Lockheed F-104 Starfighter was nicknamed the "missile with a man in it," since its long, thin fuselage and stubby wings resembled a missile more than a conventional aircraft. The F-104 was the first interceptor in the service of the United States to be able to fly at sustained speeds above Mach 2 (twice the speed of sound).

GALLERY 105. Golden Age of Flight

Aviation between the two world wars

BEECH MODEL 17 STAGGERWING. Popular general aviation aircraft of the 1930s; the museum's Staggerwing dates from 1936

WITTMAN *CHIEF OSHKOSH BUSTER.* From 1931 until its retirement in 1954, this midget air racer set records, including two wins in the Goodyear Trophy races.

CURTISS ROBIN J-1 DELUXE *OLE MISS*. Set endurance record of 27 days over Meridian, Mississippi, 1935

NORTHROP GAMMA 2B *POLAR STAR*. First flight across Antarctica, 1935

HUGHES H-1. Aircraft in which Howard Hughes set several speed records in the 1930s

GALLERY 106. Jet Aviation

The development of jet aviation and its related technology

MURAL BY KEITH FERRIS. A large-scale depiction of important jet aircraft, 1981

LOCKHEED XP-80 SHOOTING STAR *LULU BELL*. First operational US jet fighter, 1944

MESSERSCHMITT ME 262 *SCHWALBE (SWALLOW)*. World's first operational jet fighter, 1944

MCDONNELL FH-1 PHANTOM I. First US jet to take off and land on an aircraft carrier, 1947

WHITTLE W.1.X. British experimental aircraft engine that became the foundation for the American jet engine industry when it came to the United States in October 1941

HEINKEL HES 3B TURBOJET. Replica of the engine that powered the Heinkel He 178 on the world's first flight of a turbojet-powered aircraft, 1939

PRATT & WHITNEY JT9D. Turbofan engine used in wide-body jet airliners

WILLIAMS WR19. World's smallest turbofan engine

The Messerschmitt Me 262A-1a, the world's first operational jet fighter, outperformed the best Allied fighters of World War II but entered combat too late to have much impact on the war. This rare example was one of many German aircraft captured and returned to the United States for testing. It scored 42 victories over Russian aircraft and seven over American.

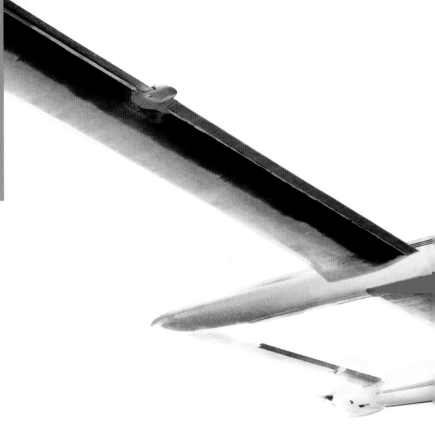

GALLERY 107. Early Flight
Crafts that evoke the mood and excitement of the dawn of flight

The Rutan *Voyager*, the first aircraft to fly nonstop around the world without refueling, is displayed in the south lobby. The *Global Flyer*, also designed by Burt Rutan, is on display at the Udvar-Hazy Center. It set several important aviation records: the first solo nonstop flight around the world; the nonstop distance record; and the closed-circuit distance record.

LILIENTHAL GLIDER. A glider built in 1894 by Otto Lilienthal, an experimenter who inspired Wilbur and Orville Wright

1909 WRIGHT MILITARY FLYER. World's first military aircraft

CURTISS D-III HEADLESS PUSHER. A favorite with US exhibition pilots in 1911–12

ECKER FLYING BOAT. Earliest existing flying boat

BLÉRIOT XI. Louis Blériot made the first heavier-than-air flight across the English Channel in a similar aircraft on July 25, 1909

LANGLEY QUARTER-SCALE AERODROME. One of several powered, unpiloted aircraft built and flown by Samuel P. Langley. This one made two successful flights, in 1901 and 1903

LANGLEY AERODROME #5. First successful flight of a powered, unpiloted heavier-than-air craft of substantial size, 1896

AERONAUTICAL ENGINES. Some of the in-line, radial, and rotary engines that propelled airplanes from 1907 to 1914

GALLERY 109. How Things Fly
A hands-on experience that explores the science behind flight in Earth's atmosphere and space

INTERACTIVE EXHIBITS. Dozens of mechanical and computer interactives demonstrate principles of flight related to air pressure and gravity, lift, drag, thrust, supersonic speed, aircraft and spacecraft control, and structures and materials.

LIVE PROGRAMS. Museum Explainers (high school and college students) bring the science of flight alive with fun experiments, unusual objects, and audience participation.

CESSNA 150. Learn how to maneuver an airplane. Climb into the cockpit of a Cessna 150 and take the controls.

THE DESIGN HANGAR. This innovative area focuses on fun, creative projects that introduce the engineering design process. Participants can imagine, plan, build, and test prototypes to overcome design challenges.

The Lockheed U-2C, an important aerial mapping and surveillance craft since the 1950s, is a focal point of the "Looking at Earth" gallery.

HOW THINGS FLY WEB SITE. Explore the physics of flight in an online experience. Test fly an aircraft, build and launch a rocket, design your own paper airplane, learn how a jet engine works, or ask a Museum Explainer a question related to air or space at howthingsfly.si.edu.

GALLERY 110. Looking at Earth
Development of technology for viewing Earth from balloons, aircraft, and spacecraft (projected closing date in 2017)

DE HAVILLAND DH-4. A British-designed and American-built World War I military aircraft later used for airmail, mapping, and photography

LOCKHEED U-2C. Key US Cold War reconnaissance aircraft, with a flight suit worn by Francis Gary Powers and memorabilia from his imprisonment in the Soviet Union; and a surveillance camera dating from the late 1950s

EARTH OBSERVATION SATELLITES. Prototype of TIROS, the world's first weather satellite, 1960; engineering test model of an ITOS weather satellite; 1970s; half-scale model of a GOES geostationary satellite and models of other satellites

LANDSAT IMAGE OF THE CHESAPEAKE BAY AREA. A 14-foot photomural, including Washington, DC, and Baltimore, Maryland

WHAT'S NEW. Developments in the science and technology of looking at Earth

GALLERY 111. Explore the Universe

How new astronomical tools—from Galileo's telescope in the early 1600s to the latest high-tech observatories on Earth and in space—have revolutionized our view of the Universe

EARLY ASTRONOMICAL TOOLS. Astrolabes, quadrants, and a celestial globe dating from 1090 to the 1600s, together with replicas of other instruments

20-FOOT TELESCOPE. The tube and mirror from the famous telescope used by William Herschel beginning in the 1700s to study the structure and nature of the Universe

OBSERVING CAGE AND CAMERA FROM THE 100-INCH TELESCOPE AT MT. WILSON OBSERVATORY IN SOUTHERN CALIFORNIA. Used by astronomer Edwin Hubble, whose discoveries changed our understanding of the nature and motion of galaxies in the early 20th century

PRIME FOCUS SPECTROGRAPH FROM THE 200-INCH TELESCOPE AT PALOMAR OBSERVATORY IN SOUTHERN CALIFORNIA. The most sensitive camera in the world mounted on the most powerful telescope in the world, this instrument helped astronomers in the latter half of the 20th century study the most distant galaxies yet seen.

HUBBLE SPACE TELESCOPE BACKUP MIRROR. This artifact, showing the honeycomb structure that supports the mirror surface, is nearly identical to the one currently in use on the Hubble.

CCDS AND OTHER LIGHT DETECTORS. Digital detectors from a variety of significant ground-, air-, and space-based instruments that were designed to explore every facet of the Universe

SPACE INSTRUMENTS. These are actual instruments returned from the Hubble, plus full-scale engineering models and originals of the suite of instruments that mapped the big bang from the ground and from space.

This type of basket, held aloft by a hot-air balloon, was used in early aerial photography. The basket is in the "Looking at Earth" gallery.

AT A GLANCE

The 1903 Wright Flyer, Charles Lindbergh's *Spirit of St. Louis,* John Glenn's *Friendship 7,* the Apollo 11 command module *Columbia,* and the walk-through Skylab orbital workshop are just a few of the attractions in this vast and exciting museum. Not to be missed are special IMAX® films projected on a screen five stories high and seven stories wide, providing a breathtaking cinematic experience.

Above: The Apollo 11 command module *Columbia* carried astronauts Neil Armstrong, Edwin "Buzz" Aldrin, and Michael Collins on their historic voyage to the Moon and back, July 16-24, 1969. Opposite: Lunar Module 2 is one of two remaining lunar landers built for the early Apollo missions.

GALLERY 112. Lunar Exploration Vehicles
Exploring the Moon

SURVEYOR LUNAR PROBE. Soft-landed on the Moon to study lunar soil composition and physical properties of the lunar surface, 1966–68

LUNAR ORBITER. Circled the Moon and mapped the entire lunar surface, 1966–67

RANGER LUNAR PROBE. Provided the first close-up photographs of the lunar surface, 1962–65

CLEMENTINE. Backup for the robotic return to the Moon, 1994

GALLERY 113. Moving Beyond Earth
Explore the opportunities and challenges of human spaceflight on the shuttle, space station, and beyond.

DISCOVER. What does it take to make a spacecraft reusable? How do astronauts spend their days on the International Space Station? What was life like on the space shuttle? What are the future plans for space transportation and exploration?

LARGE-SCALE MODEL OF SPACE SHUTTLE. Depicts the orbiter, external tank, solid rocket boosters, and mobile launch platform

SPACE SHUTTLE MID-DECK MOCKUP. See where shuttle astronauts lived and worked.

GOOGLE EARTH STATION. Explore Earth, Moon, and Mars in an immersive, interactive display.

FLIGHT SUITS. Worn by shuttle astronauts

SPACE TOOLS. Used to repair the Hubble Space Telescope

MODELS OF NEXT-GENERATION SPACECRAFT. Dragon, Orion, and others as they evolve

INTERACTIVE ACTIVITIES. Try your skills as a mission flight director or space station designer and see how much you know about spaceflight.

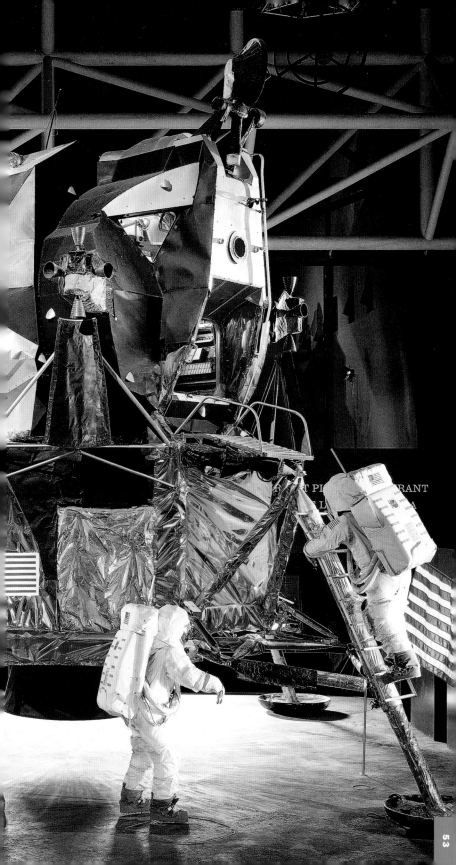

The "Space Race" gallery compares US and Soviet technology developed for manned lunar missions. At the left is a model of the US Saturn V rocket and an Apollo space suit worn on the Moon. At the right is a model of the Soviet N-1 rocket, which failed in test flights, and a Soviet Moon suit designed for a lunar landing mission that never occurred. Opposite: The "Space Race" gallery contains many artifacts from the US and Soviet space pro-grams. From left to right are the huge Skylab Or-bital Workshop, a German V-2 missile, a cluster of rockets and missiles, and the Apollo-Soyuz Test Program display.

GALLERY 114. Space Race

Tells the story of the United States' and the Soviet Union's competition in space and the race to the Moon

V-2. First operational long-range ballistic missile (German), 1944–45

AEROBEE 150. Major carrier of scientific instruments for probing the upper atmosphere, 1955–70

VIKING. US Navy sounding rocket developed for scientific purposes, 1949–55

JUPITER-C AND VANGUARD ROCKETS. First two US satellite launch vehicles, 1958

SCOUT-D. Solid-propellant launch vehicle for scientific satellites, 1961–94

MINUTEMAN III. US Air Force intercontinental ballistic missile, 1970 to the present

IVAN IVANOVICH, TEST FLIGHT MANNEQUIN. Sent into space by the Soviet space program a few weeks before the first human flight, March 1961

YURI GAGARIN FLIGHT SUIT. Worn during training by cosmonaut Yuri Gagarin, first person in space, 1961

JOHN GLENN SPACE SUIT. Worn by astronaut John Glenn, first American to orbit Earth, February 1962

SPACE SUIT AND AIRLOCK FROM FIRST SPACEWALK. Cosmonaut Aleksei Leonov became the first human to "walk" in space, March 1965

APOLLO 15 LUNAR SUIT. Astronaut David Scott wore this suit on the Moon, 1971

CORONA CAMERA. This and similar US cameras observed the Soviet Union from space, 1960–72

SKYLAB ORBITAL WORKSHOP. A walk-through backup for the first US space station, 1973–74

APOLLO-SOYUZ TEST PROJECT. First human interna-tional space mission, 1975

HUBBLE SPACE TELESCOPE. Full-size engineering model of observatory put in orbit by the space shuttle, 1990

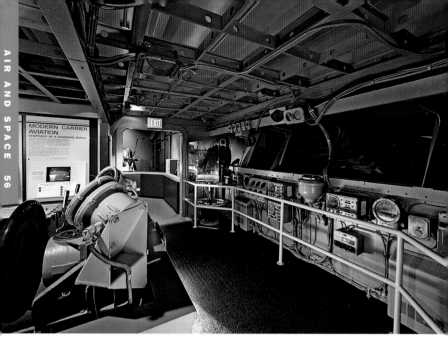

The history of ship-based flight is told in the "Sea-Air Operations" gallery. Step aboard the simulated aircraft carrier USS *Smithsonian*, CVM-76, and visit the bridge, where you can observe aircraft catapulting off the bow.

GALLERY 115. Lockheed Martin IMAX® Theater
Large-format films are shown on a screen five stories high and seven stories wide. Admission fee. Schedule available at Welcome Center.

GALLERY 201. Albert Einstein Planetarium
Lectures on the night sky and multimedia programs on astronomy and space are presented in the domed theater. The planetarium projector simulates the nighttime sky and the motions of the Sun, Moon, and planets. Admission fee for most shows.

GALLERY 203. Sea-Air Operations
Aircraft carrier operations from 1911 to the present
CARRIER HANGAR DECK. Major aircraft from different periods in sea-air history
BOEING F4B-4. Biplane built for the US Navy and Marine Corps
DOUGLAS SBD-6 DAUNTLESS. Type of carrier-based dive bomber used during most of World War II
GRUMMAN FM-1 WILDCAT. Basic US Navy and Marine Corps fighter aircraft at the start of World War II
DOUGLAS A-4C SKYHAWK. First-line naval attack aircraft of the 1950s and 1960s

CARRIER WAR IN THE PACIFIC. Depicts the six major aircraft-carrier battles in the Pacific during World War II
MODERN CARRIER AVIATION. Developments in carrier construction, operations, roles, and missions in the nuclear age

GALLERY 205. World War II Aviation
Fighter aircraft and related material from five countries
NORTH AMERICAN P-51D MUSTANG. An outstanding fighter airplane, used in every theater of the war
MITSUBISHI A6M5 ZERO FIGHTER. With excellent maneuverability and range, used throughout the war by the Japanese navy
SUPERMARINE SPITFIRE MARK VII. A later version of the legendary British fighter that helped defeat the Germans in the Battle of Britain
MESSERSCHMITT BF 109 *GUSTAV*. Principal Luftwaffe fighter and the major opponent of Spitfires, Mustangs, and US bombers
MACCHI C.202 FOLGORE. Most successful Italian fighter to see extensive service in the African campaign and in Italy and the Soviet Union
MURAL. *Fortresses Under Fire,* by Keith Ferris, 1976

The North American P-51D Mustang escorted high-altitude Allied bombers deep into Europe.

The Grumman FM-1 Wild-cat was the Navy's main carrier fighter for the first two years of World War II. This version has a mechanism that allows the wings to fold back against the fuselage for a compact fit on the flight deck.

GALLERY 206. Legend, Memory, and the Great War in the Air

The emergence of air power in World War I

PFALZ D.XII. German fighter aircraft used in Hollywood films about aviation in World War I

VOISIN VIII. Early type of night bomber, 1915

SPAD XIII *SMITH IV*. French fighter aircraft flown by US ace Ray Brooks of the 22nd Aero Pursuit Squadron

FOKKER D.VII. Considered the best German fighter aircraft of World War I

ALBATROS D.VA. German fighter aircraft that flew on all fronts during World War I

SOPWITH SNIPE. British aircraft considered to be one of the best all-around single-seat fighters, although it became operational only late in the war

GERMAN FACTORY SCENE. World War I mass-production techniques, with original equipment

HOLLYWOOD FILMS PORTRAYING A ROMANTIC IMAGE OF THE "KNIGHTS OF THE AIR."

Outside Gallery 206.

GOSSAMER CONDOR. First successful human-powered aircraft, 1977

GALLERY 207. Exploring the Planets
History and achievements of planetary exploration, Earth based and by spacecraft

VOYAGER. Full-scale replica of the spacecraft that explored Jupiter, Saturn, Uranus, and Neptune in the 1970s and 1980s

A PIECE OF MARS. Meteorite collected in Antarctica that came from Mars

SURVEYOR 3 TELEVISION CAMERA. Retrieved from the surface of the Moon by the Apollo 12 astronauts

THREE GENERATIONS OF MARS ROVERS. Full-scale models of the Mars rovers *Spirit, Opportunity,* and *Curiosity,* plus the backup vehicle for the *Sojourner* rover *Marie Curie*

NEW HORIZONS FULL-SCALE MODEL. The first spacecraft to explore Pluto

A full-scale replica of the *Voyager* spacecraft is on display in the "Exploring the Planets" at the museum in Washington, DC.

The 1903 Wright Flyer is the centerpiece of "The Wright Brothers & The Invention of the Aerial Age" gallery.

GALLERY 208. Barron Hilton Pioneers of Flight
Famous "firsts" and record setters

LOCKHEED SIRIUS *TINGMISSARTOQ*. Flown by Charles and Anne Lindbergh on airline route-mapping flights, 1930s

LOCKHEED 5B VEGA. First solo flight across the Atlantic by a woman, Amelia Earhart, 1932

FOKKER T-2. First nonstop US transcontinental flight, 1923

PIPER J-2 CUB. A stable and economical 1937 Cub light aircraft that made flying easy to learn and afford. This Piper J-2 is the first Cub built under the Piper name. Formerly known as the Taylor Cub, the J-2 model was soon modified into the world-famous Piper J-3 Cub.

"HOOPSKIRT," LIQUID FUEL ROCKET. A 1928 invention of famed rocketry pioneer Robert Goddard

INTERACTIVE ACTIVITIES. Hands-on elements for all ages, including preschool children, throughout the gallery

BUD LIGHT SPIRIT OF FREEDOM GONDOLA. First solo flight around the world in a balloon, by Steve Fossett, 2002

HAWTHORNE C. GREY BALLOON BASKET AND EQUIPMENT. Ushered in the era of stratospheric balloon flights, 1927

DOUGLAS WORLD CRUISER *CHICAGO*. First around-the-world flight, 1924

EXPLORER II GONDOLA. In 1935, this cabin and its balloon rose to a height never before achieved and made valuable scientific observations.

BLACK WINGS: THE AMERICAN BLACK IN AVIATION. Exhibit chronicles the struggle of African Americans to earn a place in aeronautics and space flight in the United States

GALLERY 209. The Wright Brothers & The Invention of the Aerial Age
The story of how Wilbur and Orville Wright invented the airplane

1903 WRIGHT FLYER. The first heavier-than-air, powered aircraft to make a sustained, controlled flight with a pilot aboard

LETTER TO THE SMITHSONIAN. Read what Wilbur Wright wrote in 1899 in this copy of a letter to the Smithsonian asking for information about aeronautics.

STOPWATCH. The Wrights used this stopwatch to time their first flights.

ST. CLAIR BICYCLE. One of only five bicycles manufactured by the Wright brothers known to exist today

WIND TUNNEL INSTRUMENT. Replica of the lift balance with which the Wrights performed their pioneering wind-tunnel research

ORIGINAL FABRIC AND PROPELLER. Both were on the Wright Flyer when it flew at Kitty Hawk in 1903.

HANDS-ON MECHANISMS. Learn about wing warping and other pioneering inventions by the Wright brothers.

FIRST FLIGHT SIMULATIONS. Watch video reenactments of the first four flights of the 1903 Wright Flyer.

Five huge F-1 rocket engines were needed to lift the 30-story-tall Saturn V rocket.

GALLERY 210. Apollo to the Moon
Triumph of human spaceflight in the 1960s and early 1970s, from Project Mercury through the Apollo Moon landings

F-1 ENGINE. Full-size, with cutaway of first-stage rocket engine used on the Saturn V rocket

SPACE TOOLS AND EQUIPMENT. Used to train for the Apollo missions

LUNAR SCENES. Showing the lunar rover and equipment deployed on the Moon's surface

LUNAR ROVER. The type of vehicle that astronauts drove on the Moon

SATURN BOOSTERS. Models of Saturn IB and Saturn V rockets

LUNAR SAMPLES. Four types of lunar soil and rocks

SPACE FOOD. How astronauts' and cosmonauts' food has changed

SPACESUITS. Worn on the Moon by Apollo astronauts

GALLERY 211. Flight in the Arts
Rotating Exhibits
GALLERY 213. Time and
Navigation
*How revolutions in timekeeping
over three centuries have influ-
enced how we find our way*

WINNIE MAE. When Wiley Post's
Lockheed Vega *Winnie Mae* circled the globe two times in the
1930s, it was a breakthrough in air
navigation.

VOLKSWAGEN TOUAREG *STANLEY.*
Car that in 2005 won the DARPA Grand Challenge
of having a vehicle navigate a complex course without a human driver

RAMSDEN DIVIDING ENGINE. This engine ultimately led
to mass production of precision octants and sextants.

MARINER 10. A Flight-Qualified Spare of the Mariner
10, a spacecraft that used a gravitational assist from
Venus to fly by Mercury three times in 1974 and 1975

SHIP'S INERTIAL NAVIGATION SYSTEM (SINS). A system of gyroscopes, accelerometers, and computers
that was used to steer submarines

Above: Using a rover like
this one, Apollo 17 astronauts spent a record 22
hours exploring the lunar
surface and collecting
rock and soil samples.
Below: *Mural Master
Study: Horizontal* by
Robert T. McCall, 1975,
acrylic on canvas, 23 x
90 in. (58 x 229 cm).

STEVEN F. UDVAR-HAZY CENTER

The National Air and Space Museum's location in
Chantilly, Virginia, offers a unique museum experience,
with artifacts displayed in a massive open setting and
organized in thematic groupings.

The ten-story Boeing Aviation Hangar contains aircraft suspended on two levels from the building's huge
trusses, with larger aircraft on the floor. The suspended
vehicles replicate their typical flight maneuvers: an aerobatic airplane hot-dogging upside down, a World War II
fighter angling for a victory, and a small two-seater flying
level. Walkways rising four stories above the floor provide nose-to-nose views of aircraft in suspended flight.

The James S. McDonnell Space Hangar is dominated
by the dramatically lit space shuttle *Discovery*, around
which hundreds of other space artifacts are arranged.
A free-floating simulated astronaut appears to be performing a spacewalk above, and oddly shaped satellites
and sleek rockets dot the overhead space. The hangar
features three elevated overlooks that allow visitors to
study suspended artifacts up close and get a view of the
entire hangar.

The Donald D. Engen Observation Tower contains
interactive flight-control displays and gives visitors a

great place to observe aircraft taking off and landing at the adjacent Washington Dulles International Airport.

Outside the Udvar-Hazy Center, the Wall of Honor leads from the parking lot to the building's entrance. Panels are engraved with the names of those who have contributed to the nation's heritage in aviation and space exploration. A polished steel sculpture by John Safer, reaching 70 feet in the air, anchors the Wall of Honor.

The artifacts listed below are only a sample of those on view.

THE BOEING AVIATION HANGAR
PRE-1920 AVIATION

CAUDRON G.4. The museum's G.4, a craft used for reconnaissance, as a bomber, and in training, is one of only two that still exist.

Above: The James S. McDonnell Space Hangar is 80 feet high, 262 feet long, and 180 feet wide. Below: The National Aviation and Space Exploration Wall of Honor on the walkway leading to the Udvar-Hazy Center honors those who have contributed to our nation's aviation and space exploration.

NIEUPORT 28. America's first fighter airplane, the Nieuport was a French design flown by US pilots in World War I.

BUSINESS AVIATION

LEARJET 23. The Model 23s were the founding products of the original Lear Jet Corporation and other pioneers in the field of business and personal jet aviation.

BEECHCRAFT KING AIR. Introduced in 1964, the King Air is the world's most popular turboprop business aircraft.

SPORT AVIATION

ARLINGTON SISU 1A. The first motorless aircraft to fly beyond 620 miles during a single flight, 1964

MONNETT MONI. John Monnett designed this motor glider in the early 1980s. It could zip along at 120 mph or glide around in search of thermal updrafts.

INTERWAR MILITARY AVIATION

BOEING P-26A PEASHOOTER. This airplane introduced the concept of the high-performance, all-metal monoplane fighter design, which was a radical departure from wood-and-fabric biplanes.

LOENING OA-1A *SAN FRANCISCO* AMPHIBIAN. Flown on the historic Pan-American Goodwill Flight of 1926 and 1927 through Mexico and Central and South America

The Caudron G.4 on display at the Udvar-Hazy Center is one of only two that still exist.

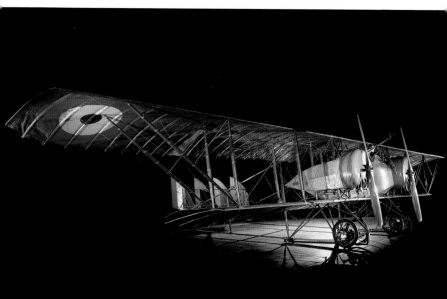

ULTRALIGHT AIRCRAFT

COSMOS PHASE II. A conservation group called Operation Migration, dedicated to replenishing the number of endangered birds, used this ultralight two-seater to lead flocks along new migration routes from Canada to the United States

ULTRALIGHT LAZAIR SS EC. This was one of the first twin-engine

ultralights, the configuration of which marked an important step in increasing the reliability of these simple and inexpensive aircrafts.

VERTICAL FLIGHT

AUTOGIRO COMPANY OF AMERICA AC-35. In 1935, this "roadable" gyroplane was a model for a suburban commuter aircraft. With folding blades and a powered drive wheel, it could do 25 mph on city streets and 90 mph in the air.

BELL H-13J. In 1957, this aircraft became the first presidential helicopter. Its primary role was to evacuate the president in case of nuclear attack.

BELL XV-15 TILT ROTOR RESEARCH AIRCRAFT. First flown in 1977, the XV-15 was the first successful tilt rotor aircraft. It could hover as a helicopter, but when converted to an airplane, it had much greater speed and range than was possible as a helicopter.

Above, front to back: The Bell Model 30 Ship 1A "Genevieve," Bell Model 47B, and Bell H-13J helicopters are now on display at the Udvar-Hazy Center. The Bell H-13J was the first helicopter to carry a US president. Below: The experimental XV-15 tilt rotor was donated by NASA and the US Army and is featured in the museum's peerless vertical flight collection at the Udvar-Hazy Center.

The Pitts Special *Little Stinker* hangs inverted above the walkway leading to the Boeing Aviation Hangar at the Steven F. Udvar-Hazy Center.

AEROBATIC FLIGHT

LOUDENSLAGER LASER 200. Between 1975 and 1982, in this airplane, Leo Loudenslager accomplished the unprecedented by winning seven US National Aerobatic Championship titles plus the 1980 World Champion title.

PITTS SPECIAL S-1C *LITTLE STINKER.* With the Pitts Special, Betty Skelton won the International Feminine Aerobatic Championships in 1949 and 1950.

GENERAL AVIATION

PIPER J-3 CUB. Thousands of private pilots, including many in the Civilian Pilot Training Program before World War II, learned to fly in this easy-to-fly, inexpensive airplane.

CESSNA 180 *SPIRIT OF COLUMBUS.* Flying this airplane in 1964, Jerrie Mock became the first woman to pilot an aircraft around the world.

COMMERCIAL AVIATION

BOEING 307 STRATOLINER. The museum's *Clipper Flying Cloud,* flown by Pan American Airways, is the only surviving Stratoliner, the first airliner to have a pressurized fuselage.

CONCORDE. The museum's Concorde, the first supersonic airliner to enter scheduled service, was the first in the Air France fleet.

BOEING 367-80. The "Dash 80" was the original prototype for the Boeing 707, America's first jetliner and the airplane that opened the world to faster, less-expensive air travel.

WORLD WAR II AVIATION

BOEING B-29 SUPERFORTRESS *ENOLA GAY.* On August 6, 1945, the *Enola Gay* dropped the first atomic bomb used in combat, on Hiroshima, Japan.

CURTISS P-40E WARHAWK. The P-40, which wore a shark-mouth paint scheme, was one of the best-known US fighters of World War II. Its greatest fame was with the Flying Tigers.

ARADO AR 234 B-2 BLITZ (LIGHTNING). The German Arado Ar 234 B Blitz was the world's first operational jet bomber and reconnaissance aircraft.

VOUGHT F4U-1D CORSAIR. The F4U Corsair, the distinctive bent-wing fighter-bomber, was both land and

carrier based. It earned a distinguished combat record in World War II and Korea.

GRUMMAN F6F-3 HELLCAT. The Hellcat, introduced in 1943, gave American pilots an aircraft that was faster and almost as maneuverable as those used by their Japanese opponents.

LOCKHEED P-38J LIGHTNING. The unique, twin-boom, twin-engine P-38 Lightning was one of the most versatile fighters of World War II.

AICHI M6A1 SEIRAN (CLEAR SKY STORM). The only surviving example of a Japanese bomber that could operate exclusively from a submarine

VOUGHT-SIKORSKY XR-4C. The culmination of Igor I. Sikorsky's attempts to create a practical helicopter, the XR-4C (1942) was the prototype for the world's first mass-produced helicopter.

COLD WAR AVIATION

LOCKHEED SR-71 BLACKBIRD. On its final flight in 1990, this Blackbird set a transcontinental speed record by flying from the West Coast to the East Coast in 64 minutes and 20 seconds.

MCDONNELL F-4S PHANTOM II. One of the most versatile military aircraft ever built and flown by the US Air Force, Marine Corps, and Navy

Above: The Air France Concorde F-BVFA, the oldest of the Air France supersonic fleet, is on display in the Commercial Aviation section. Below: The Blackbird's performance and operational achievements placed it at the pinnacle of aviation technology developments during the Cold War.

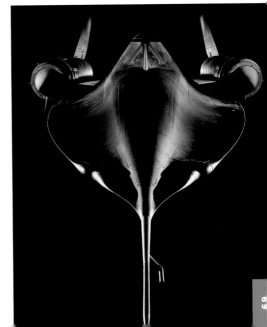

In addition to its high performance, the F-86A Sabre had excellent handling characteristics and was well liked by its pilots.

KOREA AND VIETNAM

NORTH AMERICAN F-86A SABRE. Above Korea, American pilots flying the Sabre established a significant victory ratio over enemy MiG-15s.

BELL UH-1H IROQUOIS (HUEY). What the jeep was to Americans in World War II, the Huey was to those who fought in Vietnam. People knew it not just on sight but also by the unmistakable whop-whop-whop of the main rotor blade.

REPUBLIC F-105 THUNDERCHIEF. Designed as a single-seat fighter-bomber capable of carrying nuclear weapons or heavy bomb loads at supersonic speeds

MODERN MILITARY AVIATION

LOCKHEED MARTIN JOINT STRIKE FIGHTER. A stealthy, multirole fighter, this aircraft was the first to achieve a short takeoff, level supersonic dash, and vertical landing in a single flight.

MIKOYAN-GUREVICH MIG 21F-13 FISHBED-C. The MiG-21, which entered service in 1960, was the Soviet Union's first truly modern second-generation jet fighter.

GRUMMAN F-14D(R) TOMCAT. A supersonic, twin-engine, two-place strike fighter that gave legendary service to the US Navy, the Tomcat was featured in the film *Top Gun* (1986) starring Tom Cruise.

LIGHTER-THAN-AIR FLIGHT

THE GOODYEAR *PILGRIM* BLIMP CONTROL CAR. First modern Goodyear blimp

DOUBLE EAGLE II. First balloon to fly the Atlantic

BREITLING ORBITER 3. First balloon to fly nonstop around the world

RED BULL STRATOS GONDOLA. Set world records for altitude and the highest parachute jump

AIRCRAFT ENGINES

A collection of aircraft engines is on display at ground level at the northeast end of the museum.

SMALL ARTIFACTS

Hundreds of artifacts and artifact collections, including aerial cameras, awards and insignias, machine guns, aircraft models, popular culture items, and pilot uniforms are displayed in glass cases.

Left: Pegasus was the first aircraft-launched rocket booster to carry satellites into space. Scores of missiles and rockets are displayed in the James S. McDonnell Space Hangar at the Udvar-Hazy Center. Below: The Manned Maneuvering Unit gave astronauts mobility for extravehicular activities outside the space shuttle. It now hovers over *Discovery.*

THE JAMES S. MCDONNELL SPACE HANGAR

ROCKETS AND MISSILES

GODDARD 1935 A-SERIES ROCKET. One in a pioneering series that Robert Goddard launched near Roswell, New Mexico, this artifact is the first rocket to have entered the Smithsonian collections.

CORPORAL MISSILE. The Corporal was the first nuclear-armed ballistic missile deployed by the US Army.

REDSTONE MISSILE. NASA modified the US Army's Redstone ballistic missile to send America's first astronaut—Alan Shepard—into space in 1961.

PEGASUS. This three-stage rocket was used by commercial, government, and international customers to deploy small satellites into low Earth orbit.

AGENA-B UPPER-STAGE LAUNCH VEHICLE. Agena-Bs were used from 1959 until the mid-1980s as orbital injection vehicles or intermediate stage boosters for space probes.

HUMAN SPACEFLIGHT

SPACE SHUTTLE *DISCOVERY.* The longest-serving orbiter, *Discovery* flew 39 times from 1984 through 2011—more missions than any of its sister ships—spending altogether 365 days in space.

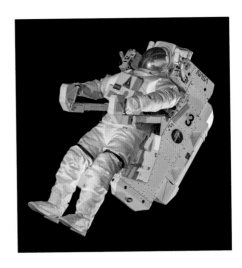

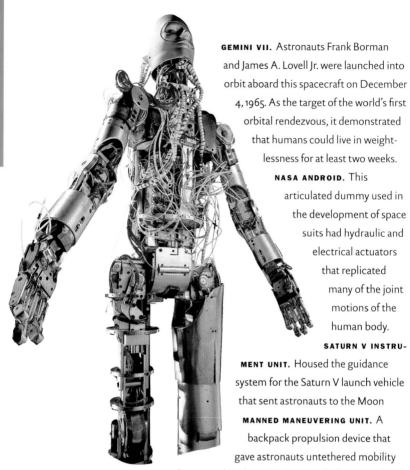

GEMINI VII. Astronauts Frank Borman and James A. Lovell Jr. were launched into orbit aboard this spacecraft on December 4, 1965. As the target of the world's first orbital rendezvous, it demonstrated that humans could live in weightlessness for at least two weeks.

NASA ANDROID. This articulated dummy used in the development of space suits had hydraulic and electrical actuators that replicated many of the joint motions of the human body.

SATURN V INSTRUMENT UNIT. Housed the guidance system for the Saturn V launch vehicle that sent astronauts to the Moon

MANNED MANEUVERING UNIT. A backpack propulsion device that gave astronauts untethered mobility for extravehicular activities outside the space shuttle

SPACE SCIENCE "ANITA." A spider flown on Skylab for web-formation experiments

MARS PATHFINDER. Test model of the spacecraft that landed on the Red Planet in July 1997 by resting on its deflated protective airbags

RITCHEY MIRROR GRINDING MACHINE. Designed in the 1890s, this device demonstrated how extremely large telescope mirrors could be fabricated.

VEGA PROBE. An engineering model of the Soviet spacecraft that flew by Venus in June 1985 and launched scientific instruments into the planet's atmosphere

APPLICATIONS SATELLITES

CORONA BUCKET. This "bucket," a film return capsule recovered on May 25, 1972, from the last CORONA photoreconnaissance satellite mission, brought back

Above: A human-sized, NASA-built android used for 1960s space suit testing is displayed in the Space Hangar at the Udvar-Hazy Center.

photos of the Soviet Union and other countries taken from space.

APPLICATIONS TECHNOLOGY SATELLITE 1. The first of a series of six satellites sponsored by NASA for research in the new field of space communications

COMPUTER, MASSIVELY PARALLEL PROCESSOR, AND EXPANSION UNIT. Together, these three technologies revolutionized the processing of vast amounts of remote sensing data from space.

SIRIUS FM-4 SATELLITE. Since 2001, this satellite has provided more than 150 digital music and audio channels to North America.

Above: Among the hundreds of items displayed in glass cases are the helmet and gloves used in training by Apollo 15 astronaut James Irwin and boots used by Mercury astronaut Gordon Cooper.
Left: "Anita," a spider used for web formation experiments aboard Skylab, is displayed in a blue bottle.

SMALL ARTIFACTS

More than 500 small artifacts used in space, including cameras and personal gear, sounding rocket payloads, space-themed toys, and even borscht in tubes prepared for Soviet cosmonauts, are exhibited in cases throughout the hangar. The Udvar-Hazy Center also features the Mary Baker Engen Restoration Hangar, where visitors can watch museum specialists working on aircraft and spacecraft from a mezzanine overlook; the Archives Department, which is open to researchers; the Emil Buehler Conservation Laboratory; the Collections Processing Unit; and a collections storage area.

Above: This Tracking and Data Relay Satellite (TDRS) system, a constellation of three spacecraft placed into geosynchronous orbit beginning in 1983, is on display in the James S. McDonnell Space Hangar.

GENERAL INFORMATION

(For the Mall building and Udvar-Hazy Center)

LOCATIONS

The National Mall building is at Independence Avenue and 6th Street, SW. Entrances: Independence Avenue and Jefferson Drive (on the Mall). The Steven F. Udvar-Hazy Center is near Washington Dulles International Airport at 14390 Air and Space Museum Parkway, Chantilly, Virginia. The entrance is off Route 28.

HOURS

Open daily from 10:00 A.M. to 5:30 P.M. Closed on December 25.

GETTING THERE

• PUBLIC TRANSPORTATION: The closest Metrorail stop to the National Mall building is the L'Enfant Plaza station. To get to the Udvar-Hazy Center, take Fairfax Connector's 983 bus from the Wiehle-Reston East Metro station.

Buses operate during museum hours. Fares and schedules can be found at fairfaxconnector.com or by calling 703-877-5965.

• BY CAR: The National Mall building does not have public parking, but many commercial parking lots are available in the area. Limited on-street parking includes some handicapped spaces. At the Udvar-Hazy Center, parking is available for $15 a day.

VISITOR SERVICES

For information on the museum in Washington, DC, call 202-633-2214. For the Udvar-Hazy Center, call 703-572-4118. Send queries by e-mail to NASM-Visitor Services@si.edu or visit the museum's Web site airandspace.si.edu.

TOURS

Highlight tours are given by museum docents daily at 10:30 A.M. and 1:00 P.M. at both locations.
SCHOOLS: School-group reservations for tours, programs, and science demonstrations must be made in writing at least three weeks in advance. Details are on the Web at airandspace.si.edu. For reservations, use the online form at airandspace.si.edu/tickets, call Monday through Friday 202-633-2563 (voice/tape) or e-mail asmtours@si.edu.

WHERE TO EAT

In the National Mall building: McDonald's, Boston Market, and Donato's Pizza are on the first floor, just past "Space Race" gallery. At the Udvar-Hazy Center: A McDonald's and McCafé are on the entrance level next to the store.

SHOPPING

The museum stores are on the first floor near the entrance in the National Mall building, and on the entrance level at the Udvar-Hazy Center.

THEATERS

Large-format films are presented on giant screens in IMAX® theaters at both locations. Simulations of the night sky and programs on astronomy and space are presented in the Albert Einstein Planetarium in the museum in Washington, DC. For show information or to purchase tickets, visit airandspace.si.edu or call 202-633-4629 or 1-877-932-4629.

ACCESSIBILITY INFORMATION

Both locations have access ramps and elevators. All theaters are wheelchair accessible, and most shows offer audio descriptions and/or closed captioning. Wheelchairs are available at both locations free of charge; inquire at the Welcome Centers. Tours for persons who have visual, hearing, or other impairments may be arranged at least three weeks in advance by calling 202-633-2563.

WHAT'S UP

For monthly updates on museum events, subscribe to the National Air and Space Museum's e-newsletter, What's Up, at airandspace.si.edu/WhatsUp.

The Sant Ocean Hall introduces visitors to the ocean as a dynamic global system essential to all life—past, present, and future.

NATIONAL MUSEUM OF NATURAL HISTORY

Constitution Avenue accessible entrance: at 10th Street, NW. Mall entrance: Madison Drive between 9th and 12th Streets, NW. Open daily from 10 A.M. to 5:30 P.M. Closed December 25. Dining: Atrium Café Metrorail: Smithsonian and Federal Triangle stations. Smithsonian information: 202-633-1000, TTY: 202-633-5285. mnh.si.edu

The National Museum of Natural History is dedicated to understanding the natural world and our place in it. As the nation's largest research museum, it is a treasure trove of more than 128 million natural and cultural objects. This encyclopedic collection serves as an essential resource for scientists studying earth sciences, the biological world, and human origins and cultures. Exhibitions and educational programs attract nearly seven million visitors a year to the museum's green-domed Beaux-Arts building, one of Washington's best-known landmarks.

Only a tiny portion of the vast collections is on public display. Many of the objects are housed in the Smithsonian's Museum Support Center in Suitland, Maryland, a state-of-the-art facility for storage and conservation of research collections.

Seemingly endless drawers of insects surround museum entomologists. More than 35 million insect specimens are in the museum's collection.

Behind the scenes in the laboratories and offices at the museum and support center, more than 100 scientists conduct research in association with colleagues from universities, other museums, and government agencies.

The story told in the museum's exhibit halls, through displays, interactive carts, and our dynamic volunteers is the story of our planet, from its fiery beginnings to its transformation over billions of years by a marvelous web of evolving life, including our own species. Living and nonliving, art and artifact—taken together, they reveal a wondrous and complex world.

GROUND FLOOR

A grand, two-story space, the Constitution Avenue Lobby features the museum's Easter Island ancestor figure, first put on exhibit in 1888. Q?rius (pronounced *curious),* The Coralyn W. Whitney Science Education Center is a new way for teens and tweens—and their families and educators—to connect science with everyday experiences. The 10,000-square-foot interactive, experimental learning space brings the museum's unique assets—the science, researchers, and collections—out from behind the scenes. Through conversations with scientists and interactions with thousands of authentic specimens and objects, visitors will enhance their grasp of the natural world, awaken new interests, and build skills for inquiry.

Q?rius is a technological event space where visitors get hands-on with real objects, high-tech equipment, and inspiring experts to explore their own connections to the natural and cultural world. It is part laboratory, part collections vault, part do-it-yourself garage, and part town square—where visitors can experience natural history in a whole new way: as alive, fun, relevant, and *theirs.*

The entrance to the Atrium Café and the glass elevator to the Samuel C. Johnson Theater where 2-D

An Easter Island *moai* stands sentry at a museum entrance.

The museum's African bull elephant welcomes visitors to the majestic four-story Rotunda.

and 3-D IMAX® films are shown can be found in the wide hallway beyond the lobby.

Baird Auditorium, used for lectures, concerts, films, and other special events, is also located on the ground floor. Just outside the auditorium, Baird Gallery displays nearly 300 mounted species of birds of the eastern United States.

FIRST FLOOR

ROTUNDA

Dominating the Rotunda is the largest mounted elephant in the world. This African bull elephant stands 13 feet 2 inches high at the shoulder and weighed close to 12 tons when alive. Surrounding the elephant, visitors can look into a miniature diorama of the elephant in its natural habitat, feel the low rumbles normally unheard by humans that elephants make to communicate over many miles, see how elephants are related to their distant, now extinct ancestors, and learn about elephant conservation efforts. The visitor information desk and IMAX® ticket sales are located just under the shadow of the elephant.

On the second-floor balcony encircling the Rotunda, interpretive exhibits look more closely at the elephant's anatomy, evolution, and role in African culture.

The eight-sided Rotunda is one of Washington, DC's most dramatic spaces, and many of its distinctive design elements are best seen from the balcony.

OCEAN

From the moment visitors arrive in the Sant Ocean Hall, they find themselves in another world. A gigantic whale dives overhead, and a vast array of fossils, specimens, and habitats invites exploration. Earth, the exhibit shows, is an ocean planet, with much of its surface covered by a magnificent swath of blue. Though the ocean

The Sant Ocean Hall ambassador, Phoenix, is modeled after an actual North Atlantic right whale living in the waters off the East Coast of the United States.

spans many basins, Earth has only one ocean, and it forms a global system essential to all life on the planet—including yours!

Opened in 2008, the Sant Ocean Hall fills a magnificently restored gallery of the museum, becoming its largest exhibition ever. Ongoing research and the museum's unparalleled collections anchor the exhibits; a mix of videos, interactive displays, and new technology for exploring the ocean draws visitors of all ages.

Phoenix, a model of an actual North Atlantic right whale tracked since birth, greets visitors. Descending through the soaring, two-story atrium, she is accurate in every detail. Only about 400 whales like her are left in

Visitors discover the ocean in all its complexity and unearthly beauty in the Sant Ocean Hall.

the world. Below the giant model, a display of hunting and ceremonial artifacts from indigenous Arctic communities reflects their respect for the whale and her gifts of food, fuel, and bone. Three magnificent fossil whales nearby chart the whale's evolution and help carry visitors back to 3.5 billion years ago when the first life forms appeared in the sea. Over time, marine species rose and fell in bursts of adaptation and extinction as ocean ecosystems changed—a process captured by the dramatic murals and fossils in the "Journey through Time" gallery.

Two shows play at opposite ends of the hall— one in the Ocean Explorer Theater, where visitors watch a manned submersible dive to the largely unknown sea floor, and the other on a six-foot-wide globe suspended in the "Science on a Sphere" gallery. Data from satellite observations illuminate the surface of the sphere, showing how the ocean functions as one huge global system.

The hall also invites visitors to become ocean explorers. In the open ocean, they find marine organisms living in three layers: sunlit surface, twilight zone (where food and light are scarce), and cold, dark ocean bottom. On the coastline—where humans most

"Science on a Sphere," created by the National Oceanic and Atmospheric Administration, uses a dramatic multimedia presentation to explain many of the complex aspects of the ocean.

impact the ocean—a look beneath a beach blanket reveals an amazing variety of microscopic animals wedged between grains of sand. The 1,500-gallon aquarium holds a live Indo-Pacific reef with dozens of colorful species.

HUMAN ORIGINS

Who are we? Who were our ancestors? When did they live?

The museum's groundbreaking David H. Koch Hall of Human Origins, which opened in 2010, explores these universal questions, showing how the characteristics that make us human evolved against a backdrop of dramatic climate change. The story begins six million

Above: This reconstruction of Shanidar 1, a male Neanderthal from Shanidar Cave, Iraq, was sculpted by John Gurche. Below: The exhibit displays many reproductions of Paleolithic paintings and sculptures, including the 17,000-year-old yellow "Chinese Horse" from Lascaux Cave, France.

years ago on the African continent, where the earliest humans took the first steps toward walking upright. Since then, more than a dozen species of early humans have existed, with multiple species often sharing the earth. All of them are now extinct—except for our own, *Homo sapiens.*

The hall tells this incredible story through more than 280 fossils, casts, and artifacts, many from the museum's own collections. Displayed alongside the research of the Smithsonian Human Origins program and other scientific institutions, the objects trace the evolutionary history of our small branch of the tree of life.

Visitors enter the hall through a time tunnel, seeing nine early human species appear and disappear and environments come and go. Along one large wall, a dramatic display of fossils, objects, videos, and images features some of the most significant "milestones" in our path to becoming human: walking upright, making tools, evolving different body types and larger brains, developing social networks, and creating symbols and language.

Three displays re-create specific moments in the past and invite visitors to explore actual excavations. The braincase of a 1.8-million-year-old youth found in Swartkrans, South Africa, for example, still shows a leopard's fatal puncture marks. Visitors reconstruct the scene as they touch models of fossil "clues" from the site, and the life-and-death events of that fateful day long ago unfold in a time-lapse animation.

At the crossroads of the hall, a fascinating display of fossil skulls illustrates the history of human evolution. Nearby, eight lifelike faces stare out at visitors. It took artist John Gurche more than two years to sculpt the faces, using the latest forensic techniques, fossil discoveries, and his knowledge of human and ape anatomy.

Our species, *Homo sapiens*, evolved in East Africa by around 200,000 years ago, and then—as a world map of fossil discoveries shows—spread around the globe. Physical and cultural differences emerged as populations adapted to different habitats. Still, despite superficial variations in size, shape, skin, and eyes, the DNA among all modern humans differs by only 0.1 percent.

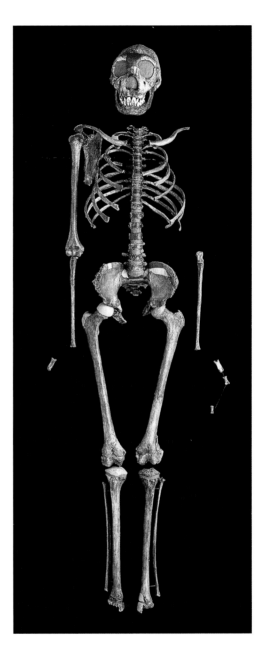

The skeleton of Turkana Boy, a juvenile *Homo erectus*, was found in 1.6-million-year-old sediments west of Lake Turkana, Kenya.

MAMMALS

The Kenneth E. Behring Family Hall of Mammals invites you to join the mammal family reunion in a dramatic hall restored to its impressive original architecture after a major renovation. The mammals hall presents the wondrous diversity of mammals and tells the story of how they adapted to a changing world. As the exhibit demonstrates, all mammals past and present—visitors included—are related to one another by virtue of common descent. Mammals belong to an ancient lineage that stretches back to the time before dinosaurs. Living mammals all share certain characteristics that scientists use to identify the group. Mammals have hair, nurse on milk, and have a unique hearing apparatus that evolved from ancestral jawbones. We are all part of the great diversity of mammals.

The hall combines a passionate and detailed commitment to scholarship with fresh interpretive approaches custom-designed to meet the needs of visitors. The exhibition features the museum's collections and takes full advantage of the exciting array of new interactive learning technologies, which allow for engaging and in-depth content. Designed with families in mind, the exhibit showcases taxidermy mammals in exciting, lifelike poses, features a wealth of hands-on

activities, and has an award-winning theater presentation on mammal evolution.

Visit the grassland, desert, and forest of Africa: get up close to a giraffe, see how lions hunt large prey, find out about bears that lived here more than five million years ago. Wander through Australia, where ancient mammals flourished and today is the only place in the world inhabited by all three mammal groups: monotremes, marsupials, and placentals. Visit North America's far north and see how mammals protect themselves from the cold. Then travel to the North American prairie and discover how the pronghorn runs faster than any other living mammal and why bison are so well suited to this environment.

Discover the world of the Amazon rain forest, the Earth's largest, where abundant plant life sets the stage for crowded living conditions. Find out how rain forest mammals make the most of these resources, from the shady forest floor to the canopy above.

If you really want to get to know your relatives, the Kenneth E. Behring Hall of Mammals is the place to go!

Above: A pouncing tiger is one of the 274 species of mammals that greet visitors to the Kenneth E. Behring Family Hall of Mammals. Opposite: North America's largest living carnivore, the brown bear looks similar to its 250,000-year-old ancestors.

Top: The *Triceratops* on display is the world's first totally digitized dinosaur. Bottom: Visitors witness the painstaking process of making casts from fragile fossils.

FOSSILS

NEW NATIONAL FOSSIL HALL, COMING IN 2019

How did life—and all its wondrous forms—come about? How is the evolution of life linked to the environmental forces at work over the history of the Earth? The new *Deep Time* exhibit in the David H. Koch Hall of Fossils will tell the history of life on a grand scale— and it is told in the exhibition taking shape in our new Fossil Hall, which is currently undergoing the largest and most complex renovation in the Museum's history as the original Beaux Arts architecture is restored and thousands of specimens are prepared so they can tell stories based on the latest scientific thinking.

Many of our most iconic fossil specimens have been on display since the museum opened in 1911. This renovation offers the opportunity to restore and remount many of our older fossil specimens, while making room for impressive recent finds. These specimens are part of the 40 million fossil animals, plants, single-celled organisms, and sediment samples in our collections, a treasure trove of evidence that our paleontologists study as they work to unravel the past.

When the hall opens, visitors will begin their exhibit journey in the recent Ice Ages, just off the Rotunda. They will peer into models of Earth's past environments and see spectacular groupings of both bizarre and familiar-looking organisms. They will learn how plants and animals in every ecosystem form an intricate web of connections, and they will see how organisms adapt, migrate, or go extinct in the face of challenges such as continental movement, asteroid strikes on Earth's surface, and climate change.

The new exhibition will explore how global environmental change affected life and ecosystems in the past and has created the world we know today. In a series of provocative displays, the exhibition will put people in the midst of the grand display of life, highlighting the crucial role we play as a worldwide geological force now and in the years ahead. Visitors will explore what this could mean for our future in the Age of Humans theater presentation and interactives.

AFRICA

Rich and resonant voices from Africa and the African diaspora—together with objects both commonplace and extraordinary—express the complexity of African lives and cultures. Africa's most striking characteristics are its immense size and diverse cultures. More than three times larger than the continental United States, Africa today is home to more than a billion people inhabiting 54 countries. The African continent is divided by the boundaries of its nation-states as well as by diverse language groups, cultures, ecological zones, and histories.

The "African Voices" exhibit resonates with the dynamism of contemporary African culture. It examines the overlapping, continuously broadening spheres of African influence—historical and contemporary, local and international—in the realms of family, work, commerce, and the natural environment. Objects such as a 17th-century cast brass head from the Benin Kingdom of Nigeria, a late-19th-century carved wooden staff by the Luba of Zaire, and decorative fiber headwear from 19th- and 20th-century Zaire show the aesthetic di-

This 18th-century brass head of an *oba*, or king, comes from the Benin Kingdom, now a part of Nigeria. The opening on top once held a carved ivory tusk depicting the glories of the *oba*'s reign.

mensions of leadership in certain African societies. A late-19th-century copper-and-brass image made by the Kota peoples of Gabon and a contemporary Afro-Brazillian altar demonstrate the enduring presence of African belief systems on the African continent and in Africa's diaspora. Akan gold weights, Ethiopian silver crosses, and decorated ceramic vessels show the history of metallurgy and pottery in different regions. Objects used in everyday life, contemporary fashion, children's toys, musical instruments, and excerpts from oral poetry, song, and literary texts illustrate the transatlantic connection between Africa and the Americas.

SECOND FLOOR

GEOLOGY, GEMS, AND MINERALS

The Janet Annenberg Hooker Hall of Geology, Gems, and Minerals, located off the second-floor Rotunda balcony, is the world's most comprehensive earth science complex. The legendary Hope diamond—a must-see for visitors—stars in the "Harry Winston" gallery. Surrounded by sparkling white diamonds, the 45.52-carat blue diamond rotates in a custom-made vault under precise fiber- optic lighting. The gem is named for former owner Henry Philip Hope of England and is still in the setting made for Evelyn Walsh McLean of

The platinum and diamond earrings of Marie Antoinette.

Washington, DC, its last private owner. The New York jewelry firm, Harry Winston, Inc., acquired the famous diamond in 1949 and donated it to the Smithsonian in 1958.

The "Harry Winston" gallery also features five other wonders of nature: enormous quartz crystals from Africa, one of the largest sheets of naturally occurring copper in existence, a sandstone formation sculpted by water within the earth, polished gneiss born from heat and pressure deep below the surface, and a ring-shaped meteorite from another world.

The "National Gem Collection" includes the Marie Antoinette earrings, the 127-carat Portuguese diamond, the Carmen Lúcia ruby, and the Hooker starburst diamonds.

The 2,500 specimens in the "Gems and Minerals" gallery include spectacular crystal pockets, a dazzling selection of gems, and crystals that have grown in amazing and unusual ways. In the "Rocks" gallery, each specimen represents a bit of Earth's history and shows how rocks bend, break, melt, and transform into other kinds of rocks over time. Intense heat from within the earth drives the movement of rocky plates at the surface—the process highlighted in the "Plate Tectonics" gallery with a giant globe, specimens from volcanoes and earthquakes, a volcano study station, and a theater. Completing the hall, the "Moon, Meteorites, and Solar System" gallery features Moon rocks, a touchable Mars meteorite, an extensive display of other meteorites, and tiny bits of stardust from the cloud that gave birth to the sun.

Above: The 45.52-carat Hope diamond is the best-known and largest blue diamond in the world. **Below:** This case houses a rare Moon rock. This display is one of a series that shows the different stages in the Moon's evolution.

BUTTERFLIES + PLANTS

No matter what season you visit, it feels like a picture-perfect summer day inside the Butterfly Pavilion. Hundreds of butterflies and moths flutter from flower to flower, sip nectar, roost, and flex their wings. Small chrysalides hang in the Transformation Station just as they would in nature while caterpillars' tissues reorganize and adult butterflies take shape. The butterflies and moths come in a stunning variety of colors and patterns, which helps protect them from predators. Look for moths that match the bark where they roost, conspicuous wing patterns that advertise a bitter taste, and eye spots on wings that help frighten away birds and lizards. Tickets for the pavilion are available online at butterflies.si.edu, by phone at 202-633-4629 or at the pavilion box office.

There is no charge to see the many other displays in "Butterflies + Plants: Partners in Evolution," where visitors discover more about how butterflies and moths live and how they evolved with plants over hundreds of millions of years. Sometimes butterflies and plants interact as friends, sometimes as foes. Take the yucca moth and yucca plant. For some 40 million years,

A rose swallowtail butterfly in profile.

yucca moths have played an active role in fertilizing yucca plants while depositing their eggs in the yucca flowers' ovaries. Milkweed plants, however, defend themselves against insect invaders with milky sap that sticks to mouthparts and bodies. Milkweed beetles have evolved a behavior that avoids the sap by cutting into leaf veins and letting the latex drain out so they can feed.

A series of murals and rare plant and insect fossils paint images of Earth in four different time periods, showing how tens of millions of years of evolution produced the amazing diversity of butterflies and moths seen today. Along the way, many species died out, while others endured, eventually giving rise to the specialized day-flying moths we now call butterflies.

A display near the Rotunda entrance gives a sense of just how large the museum's plant, insect, and fossil collections are, and the critical role they play as museum scientists work to unravel the mysteries of evolution.

The Ulysses swallowtail butterfly is native to Australia.

Above: At the popular Insect Zoo, you can get close enough to see the hairs on a tarantula. Tarantulas use the hairs to locate prey. Below: The massive skeleton of a Steller's sea cow—perhaps the most complete such skeleton in existence—looms over skeletons of meat-eating animals. It was assembled from bones salvaged on Bering Island in 1883.

INSECT ZOO

The whirls, chirps, buzzes, and rattles heard at the entrance to the Insect Zoo are the sounds of Earth's most abundant, diverse, and successful animals—insects and their relatives. They have adapted extraordinarily well to environments all over the world.

The interactive exhibits and participatory activities in the Insect Zoo invite visitors of all ages to explore and get involved. Children can crawl through a large model of an African termite mound, examine a real beehive, or hold a hissing cockroach. Tarantula feedings take place several times a day.

ANCIENT EGYPT

In "Eternal Life in Ancient Egypt," mummies, their burial wraps, and their tomb objects give visitors

dramatic evidence of life in an ancient culture that lasted for more than 3,000 years. One of the mummies on display lies in its original coffin, surrounded by various tomb objects. A gold mask and fragments of papier-mâché painted with elaborate symbols and figures ornament the head and body. Next to the mummy, visitors see jewelry, cosmetics, and a plat for food—everyday objects made of the tomb.

BONES

Hundreds of skeletons of mammals, birds, reptiles, amphibians, and fishes—ranging from a gigantic, extinct Steller's sea cow to a tiny pocket mouse—are exhibited in characteristic poses and grouped by order to illustrate their relationships. Exhibits also show how bone structures evolved in adaptation to environment. Zebras, for example, have elongated lower leg and foot bones that enable them to outrun predators on open African savannas. The massive leg bones of the hippopotamus are built to support its huge body.

View of "Eternal Life in Ancient Egypt" exhibition.

THE STORY IN THE COFFIN

AT A GLANCE

Dinosaurs, the Hope diamond, the African bull elephant, and the huge North Atlantic right whale are among the most popular exhibits of this museum. Also of special interest is Q?rius (pronounced *curious*), an interactive learning space where teens can explore thousands of authentic museum specimens and objects.

KOREA

Thousands of years ago, on a peninsula in East Asia, the distinctive culture and language of Korea arose. The Korea Gallery features several traditions that help define the country's strong national identity, using artifacts from the museum and other collections from around the world.

Elegantly presented in front of Korean latticework, a chronological display of ceramics, including classic Korean celadons, helps put Korea's long history in context. Contemporary wedding garments illustrate distinctive wedding traditions. Other displays explore Korean ancestor worship and Hangeul, the unique syllabic writing system of Korea.

Just outside the gallery, contemporary Korean art shows how the rich traditions of the past provide inspiration for a dynamic, modern Korea.

SPECIAL EXHIBITS

There's always something new to see at the museum. From world-class photography displays to fascinating archaeological finds that illuminate understanding of the past, the National Museum of Natural History offers an exciting roster of changing exhibitions every year. The exhibits amplify the museum's mission of explaining the natural world and our place in it, and they complement its research and educational goals.

The museum hosts traveling exhibits from other institutions as well as those developed by our own exhibits and curatorial staff. Many exhibitions reflect the cutting-edge science and research conducted at the museum.

FORCES OF CHANGE

Nearly every scientific and social issue confronting us today relates to change. Understanding and adapting to these changes—whether they involve climate, ecology, or culture—presents critical challenges.

The museum's "Forces of Change" program explores these complex issues by looking at the intimate and often surprising connections between seemingly unrelated natural forces. Outreach activities, a Web portal (forces.si.edu), a book, and exhibits are available. The exhibits focus on diverse topics such as El Niño, Earth's atmosphere, and the Arctic.

In every exhibit, cultural and natural objects from the museum's collections provide tangible evidence of change. Interpretive stations and computer interactives highlight current scientific research and show how the forces of nature affect our lives.

JOHNSON IMAX® THEATER

The lights go down, the show begins, and you are in another part of the world, far from Washington, DC. Perhaps you dive to the ocean depths for close encounters with some of the world's most exotic marine mammals; or you might travel back to the age of the dinosaurs, coming face-to-face with some of Earth's largest creatures ever. Whatever the topic, the theater's six-story screen, 3-D technology, and state-of-the-art sound system provide a truly memorable experience for the entire family.

The IMAX® films offered at the museum tell stories that revolve around our collections and exhibits, from oceans to dinosaurs to human evolution. The Samuel C. Johnson IMAX® Theater operates daily during regular museum hours. Schedules, feature information, and tickets are available at 202-633-IMAX (4629) and online at si.edu/imax.

Opposite top: Carved wooden *sotdae* are traditionally erected at Korean village entrances to protect the community against calamities. Opposite bottom: Smithsonian forensic anthropologist Doug Owsley examines a burial in Jamestown, Virginia. The Smithsonian's work in Jamestown is featured in the special exhibit *Written in Bone: Forensic Files of the 17th-Century Chesapeake.*

GENERAL INFORMATION

INFORMATION SERVICES

The visitor information desks, located near the Constitution Avenue entrance and in the Rotunda, are staffed by volunteers daily from 10 A.M. to 4:30 P.M. Call 202-633-3611 (voice/tape) or go online to mnh.si.edu.

TOURS

GUIDED TOURS

The National Museum of Natural History offers visitors free guided tours, interactive gallery talks, and hands-on Q?rius Carts located throughout the Museum. Tours, gallery talks, and Q?rius Carts presented by our dynamic and knowledgeable volunteers are centered on the museum's vast collections that investigates the natural world and our place in it.

FREE TOURS

"El Niño's Powerful Reach" was the Forces of Change premiere exhibit.

Highlights of the building and collections are available Monday through Friday. Check the museum's Web site or stop by the information desks. Reservations are not neccessary.

Q?RIUS CARTS

The Q?rius experience can be found in each of the museum galleries in the form of our interactive Q?rius Carts. Visitors can get an up-close look at real objects and explore their connection to the natural world alongside our expert volunteers.

THE SANT OCEAN HALL

Free gallery talks and tours of the Sant Ocean Hall are available most days; Meet at entrance to the ocean hall, first floor, just off the Rotunda.

DAVID H. KOCH HALL OF HUMAN ORIGINS

Free gallery talks and tours of the David H. Koch Hall of Human Origins are available most days; museum volunteers welcome visitors, answer questions, and help visitors navigate the exhibition.

JANET ANNENBERG HOOKER HALL OF GEOLOGY, GEMS, AND MINERALS

Free gallery talks and tours of the Janet Annenberg Hooker Hall of Geology, Gems, and Minerals are available most days; museum volunteers answer questions and engage visitors throughout the exhibition.

ACCESSIBILITY

The wheelchair-accessible entrance is at 10th and Constitution Avenue NW. Accessibility information for the Smithsonian Institution is available at si.edu/visit/visitorswithdisabilities, or by telephone at 202-633-3611. Baird Auditorium offers loop amplification in the center front rows, and assistive listening devices are available at the IMAX® and Q?rius theaters. For special services for groups, call 202-633-3611 (voice), or fax 202-786-2778.

DINING

The 600-seat Atrium Café in the Discovery Center on the ground floor offers hamburgers, hot dogs, french fries, pizza, roast chicken, pasta, submarine sandwiches, salads, ice cream, desserts, beverages, and other lunch items in a casual atmosphere. Café Natural on the ground floor offers espresso, ice cream, sandwiches, and light snacks.

MUSEUM STORES

The main museum store on the ground floor carries a variety of Smithsonian souvenirs and gifts related to natural history. Across the hall is a store especially appealing to children. Theme-oriented shops elsewhere in the museum feature books and memorabilia relating to exhibitions.

Q?RIUS JR.

On the first floor is the family-oriented education facility Q?rius jr., a discovery room for children ages 8 and under. Please consult the museum Web site for Q?rius jr. hours, programming, and other recommendations. All children visiting Q?rius jr. must be accompanied by an adult. To learn more or to register your group for a school program, visit qrius.si.edu.

Please
Don't Touch

SAMUEL C. JOHNSON IMAX® THEATER

Check the museum's Web site or call 202-633-IMAX (4629) for schedules and ticketing information. For groups, call 1-866-868-7774. For online information and sales, visit si.edu/imax.

LIVE BUTTERFLY PAVILION

Open daily 10:15 A.M. to 5 P.M. Tickets are required and are available online at butterflies.si.edu/tickets, by phone at 202-633-4629 and at the pavilion box office. Tuesdays are free, but a timed-entry ticket is required.

LIVE DEMONSTRATIONS

Tarantula feedings, Insect Zoo, Monday through Friday, 10:30 A.M., 11:30 A.M., and 1:30 P.M.; Saturday and Sunday, 11:30 A.M., 12:30 P.M., and 1:30 P.M.

Q?RIUS, THE CORALYN W. WHITNEY SCIENCE EDUCATION CENTER

Q?rius is an evolving learning lab on the ground floor of the museum. During the summer, it is open to the public daily from 10 A.M. until 5 P.M. From October through June, Q?rius is available to school groups Monday through Friday with reservations during morning hours.

In the Constitution Avenue Lobby stands a *rai*, a symbol of status on the Micronesian Island of Yap.

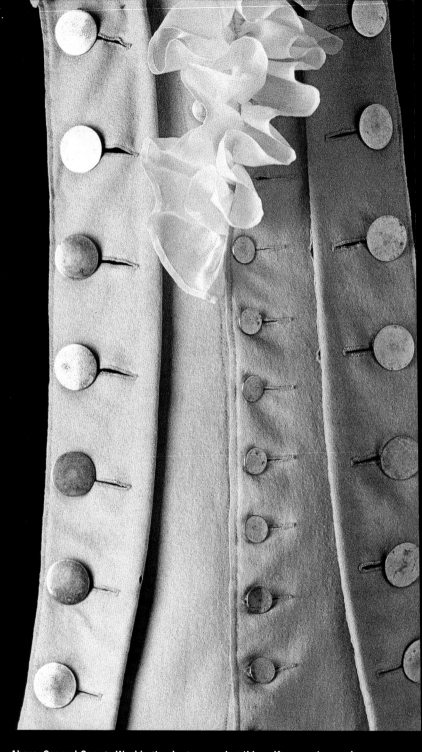

Above: General George Washington began wearing this uniform coat around 1789, after he had resigned from the Continental army to become the nation's commander in chief. Opposite top: The "Teddy bear" was created by the Ideal Toy Company and named after Theodore Roosevelt in 1903.

Constitution Avenue
between 12th
and 14th Streets, NW.
Mall entrance: Madison
Drive between 12th and
14th Streets, NW.
Open daily from
10 A.M. to 5:30 P.M.
Closed December 25.
Metrorail: Federal
Triangle or
Smithsonian station.
Smithsonian
information:
202-633-1000.
americanhistory.si.edu

NATIONAL MUSEUM OF AMERICAN HISTORY,

KENNETH E. BEHRING CENTER

In 1858, the "objects of art and of foreign and curious research" in the National Cabinet of Curiosities were transferred from the US Patent Office to the Smithsonian Institution. This was the genesis of the collections in the National Museum of American History. After the Centennial Exposition of 1876 closed, the Smithsonian received a windfall of objects that had been displayed in Philadelphia for the nation's 100th anniversary celebration. Many of those objects were put on exhibit in the US National Museum Building (now the Arts and Industries Building) when it opened in 1881. Today, the spacious halls of the National Museum of American History are filled with exhibits that explore America's social, cultural, scientific, and technological history.

The photograph shows text on the wall:

O SAY CAN YOU SE
WHAT SO PROUDLY
WHOSE BROAD STR
O'ER THE RAMPART
AND THE ROCKETS
GAVE PROOF THRO
O SAY DOES THAT
O'ER THE LAND OF

The flag that inspired the national anthem is displayed at the heart of the museum in a specially constructed gallery.

SHINING NEW LIGHT ON AMERICAN HISTORY

Visitors immediately connect to the American story as they walk into the Smithsonian's National Museum of American History's central atrium from the Mall. A skylight dramatically opens the building, and a grand staircase connects the museum's first and second floors. A Welcome Center on the second floor and an information desk on the first floor orient visitors to the museum.

The National Museum of American History has recently transformed how its audiences experience history—through new exhibitions, learning places, and programming spaces all centered on the theme of innovation. The 45,000-square-foot Innovation Wing on the first floor features exhibitions that explore the history of American business, showcase "hot spots" of invention, and put the spotlight on the National

SMITHSONIAN INSTITUTION LIBRARIES GALLERY

The Smithsonian Institution Libraries Exhibition Gallery is located on the first floor in the west wing of the National Museum

of American History. The wing will be undergoing renovation, and the Libraries Galley will close temporarily—check the NMAH Web site for dates. Guest-curated by Smithsonian staff, the exhibition showcases books from the Libraries' rich and diverse collections. For more information, see page 20.

Numismatics Collection. Updates will be posted on the museum's Web site, americanhistory.si.edu.

FIRST FLOOR

EAST WING: TRANSPORTATION AND TECHNOLOGY
WEST WING: INVENTION AND INNOVATION

AMERICA ON THE MOVE

This 26,000-square-foot exhibition anchors the General Motors Hall of Transportation and features more than 300 transportation artifacts—from the 1903 Winton that was the first car to be driven across the USA, to the 199-ton, 92-foot-long "1401" locomotive, to a 1970s shipping container—all showcased in period settings.

The exhibition's 19 settings, organized chronologically, allow visitors the opportunity to travel back in time and experience transportation as it shaped American lives and landscapes. As visitors travel through the show, they can walk on 40 feet of Route 66's original pavement from Oklahoma or board a 1950s Chicago Transit Authority Car and, through multi-media technology, experience a "commute" into downtown Chicago on a December morning.

The *Fredonia's* deep hull, narrow beam, and fine lines represent the pinnacle of design for deepwater fishing schooners. In 1896, the *Fredonia* was hit by a heavy sea and sank.

ON THE WATER

An 8,000-square-foot exhibition about the country's maritime history and culture, "On the Water: Stories from Maritime America" engages the public in a dynamic exploration of America's maritime past and present through objects, video, and interactive stations.

JOHN BULL LOCOMOTIVE
LANDMARK OBJECT – TRANSPORTATION AND TECHNOLOGY

The oldest operable self-propelled locomotive in the world, the John Bull became a symbol of the Industrial Revolution. Built in England and brought to America in 1831 for service on the Camden and Amboy Railroad of New Jersey, one of the first public railroads in the United States, the John Bull was an English design modified to fit the expansion of a frontier nation. The locomotive transported passengers from two of America's largest cities, Philadelphia and New York.

WARNER BROS. THEATER
FIRST FLOOR CENTER, NEAR THE CONSTITUTION AVE ENTRANCE

The Warner Bros. Theater is a state-of-the-art venue for public programs, including film screenings, lectures, concerts, and symposia. The theater hosts *We the People,* a special film that provides visitors a broad overview of the history of America. Check the information desk or visit the museum's Web site for the current schedule.

LIGHTING A REVOLUTION

Thomas Edison's revolutionary invention is only the beginning of the story of electricity, which is the subject of this exhibition. Here, visitors can explore the similarities and differences between the processes of invention in Edison's era and today.

The John Bull was a symbol of the Industrial Revolution and an engine of change. Built in England and brought to America in 1831, the John Bull is the world's oldest operable self-propelled locomotive. The Bull transported passengers from Philadelphia and New York City and set the style for American locomotives to come.

POWER MACHINERY

The full-size engines and models displayed here illustrate the harnessing of atmospheric forces, the early age of steam power, and the development of high-pressure and high-speed engines. Displays show the evolution of steam boilers and the steam turbine, and progress in the techniques of harnessing waterpower. The collection also includes a number of historic internal-combustion engines.

STORIES ON MONEY

"Stories on Money" explores the museum's National Numismatic Collection through two different themes. "America's Money," featuring objects from colonial America and the gold rush, examines how money changed from colonial days to the present and explores the renaissance of American coinage. "The Power of Liberty" presents an array of liberty coins from the United States and around the world as well as coins featuring real and mythological women. The exhibition immerses visitors in objects and interactive media through which they can view enlarged images and delve into numismatic history.

FOOD: TRANSFORMING THE AMERICAN TABLE 1950–2000 & JULIA CHILD'S KITCHEN

This exhibition examines some of the major changes in food and wine in postwar America. From the impact of new technologies to the influence of social and cultural shifts, the exhibition considers how these factors helped transform food and its production, preparation, and consumption as well as what we know about what's good for us. The public is invited to take a seat at a large communal table in the center of the exhibition to share thoughts and experiences about food and change in America. Julia Child's home kitchen, with its hundreds of tools, appliances, and furnishings, serves as the opening story of the museum's first major exhibition on food history.

A Thomas Edison light-bulb, early 1880.

This ten dollar coin was made in 1850 by Baldwin & Company during the gold rush. The cowboy design celebrates the spirit of the western frontier.

AT A GLANCE

The Star-Spangled Banner, the first ladies' gowns, Abraham Lincoln's hat, Lewis and Clark's compass, Muhammad Ali's boxing gloves, Thomas Jefferson's portable wooden desk on which he wrote the Declaration of Independence, the John Bull locomotive—the list of America's favorites goes on and on in the museum's wide-ranging, entertaining, and educational collections.

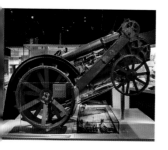

A Fordson tractor in "American Enterprise."

On the west side of the building, explore the museum's new Innovation Wing, which has more than a dozen exhibitions, hands-on learning spaces, and places for programs.

RALPH BAER'S INVENTOR'S WORKSHOP
LANDMARK OBJECT – 1 WEST

Ralph H. Baer, known as the inventor of the home video game, donated his workshop to the museum. "Innovation Nation" introduces visitors to the theme of innovation through gaming technology.

INVENTING IN AMERICA
JOHNSON LOUIS GATEWAY TO INNOVATION

The introduction to the theme of innovation begins in the concourse area leading to the west wing. Here, in collaboration with the US Patent and Trademark Office, "Inventing in America" focuses on inventions and innovators of the past and present, including Alexander Graham Bell, Thomas Edison, and Samuel Morse. The display features early patent models as well as trademarks and inventions of National Inventors Hall of Fame members.

AMERICAN ENTERPRISE
MARS HALL OF AMERICAN BUSINESS

"American Enterprise" chronicles the tumultuous interaction of capitalism and democracy that resulted in the continual remaking of American business—and American life. Visitors are immersed in the dramatic arc of power, wealth, success, and failure in America in an 8,000-square-foot space centered on the role of business and innovation from the mid-1700s to the present and tracing the country's development from a small, dependent, agricultural nation to one of the world's most vibrant economies. In addition to a chronological and thematic approach, the exhibition focuses on advertising history and features a biography wall with inventors, entrepreneurs, marketers, regulators, and others who have influenced and changed the marketplace. The show concludes with "The Ex-

change," a section of the exhibition with interactive and hands-on opportunities for visitors.

SPARK!LAB

Spark!Lab is where museum visitors become inventors. The Lemelson Center for the Study of Invention and Innovation invites children ages 6–12 to create, collaborate, explore, test, experiment, and invent. Activities for children and families incorporate traditional science, technology, engineering, and math (STEM) with art, museum activities, and creativity.

SECOND FLOOR

EAST WING: AMERICAN IDEALS
WEST WING: AMERICAN LIVES
STAR-SPANGLED BANNER GALLERY

The museum is home to the Star-Spangled Banner, the flag that inspired the national anthem. Visitors are able to view the flag in an atmosphere reminiscent of the "dawn's early light"—what Francis Scott Key experienced on the morning of September 14, 1814 and learn about history and preservation.

Above: Live cooking demonstrations! Check the museum's Web site for current schedule. Below: The first floor of the west wing focuses on innovation and creativity. The Manchester, New Hampshire, workshop of Ralph H. Baer, a prolific inventor who is often referred to as the "father of video games," is the landmark object here.

In Spark!Lab, children create, collaborate, explore, test, experiment, and invent.

"Places of Invention," one of the exhibitions featured in the Innovation Wing.

PLACES OF INVENTION
JEROME AND DOROTHY LEMELSON HALL
OF INVENTION AND INNOVATION

"Places of Invention" takes visitors on a journey through time and place across America to discover the stories of six inspiring communities. A focus on precision manufacturing in Hartford, Connecticut, in the late 1800s shows how a factory town puts the pieces together in explosive new ways. The story of Technicolor in Hollywood, California, in the 1930s puts the spotlight on the young town that gave birth to the golden age of movies. An examination of cardiac innovations of the 1950s in Medical Alley, Minnesota, reveals how a tight-knit community of tinkerers keeps hearts ticking. A look at hip-

hop's birth in the Bronx, New York, in the 1970s shows how neighborhood ingenuity created new beats. The rise of the personal computer in Silicon Valley, California, in the 1970s–80s reminds us how suburban garage hackers plus lab researchers equaled personal computing. Through clean-energy innovations in Fort Collins, Colorado, a college town combines its energies for a greener planet.

INVENTIVE MINDS
JEROME AND DOROTHY LEMELSON HALL OF INVENTION AND INNOVATION

"Inventive Minds," adjacent to "Places of Invention," introduces visitors to the mission and work of the Lemelson Center, particularly its efforts to document invention. Brief video interviews of inventors, complemented by archival materials and artifacts, puts the focus on the people, who tell their stories in their own words—and their processes. The gallery also highlights the inventive creativity of Jerome Lemelson and the vision of Lemelson and his wife, Dorothy, in founding the Lemelson Center at the Smithsonian in 1995.

"Object Project," an exhibition about everyday things that changed everything.

PATRICK F. TAYLOR FOUNDATION "OBJECT PROJECT"

On view here are everyday things that changed everything. "Object Project" presents familiar objects in a new light, exploring how people, innovations, and social change shaped life as we know it. Visitors have the opportunity to see and handle objects—from refrigerators and bicycles to ready-to-wear clothing and household conveniences as diverse as window screens and deodorant—and explore their significance through historic documents and compelling activities. Encompassing almost 4,000 square feet, the display features some 300 objects, including a "magic" scrapbook and a special version of "The Price Is Right," and offers visitors the chance to try on clothing virtually.

WEGMANS WONDERPLACE

This space allow curious kids ages 5 and under to "cook" in a kitchen inspired by Julia Child; plant and harvest pretend vegetables and run the farm stand; find the owls hiding in a miniature replica of the Smithsonian's Castle building; and captain a tugboat based on a model in the museum's collection. Here we nurture the motivation behind innovation—the sense of wonder that causes us to ask why . . . or why not.

DOLLHOUSE

Faith Bradford donated this dollhouse to the Smithsonian in 1951 after spending more than a half century collecting and building its miniature furnishings. The house is inhabited by Peter Doll, his wife, Rose Washington Doll, and their ten children.

THE VALUE OF MONEY GALLERY OF NUMISMATICS

A vault door marks the entrance to "The Value of Money," where visitors delve into the National Numismatic Collection to explore the origins of money, new monetary technologies, the political and cultural messages money conveys, numismatic art and design, and the practice of collecting money. Featuring more than 400 objects from the collection, including a storied 1933 Double Eagle, a personal check signed by President James Madison in 1813, a 1934 $100,000 dollar note, and a depression-era one-dollar clamshell.

WALLACE H. COULTER PERFORMANCE PLAZA

Against the backdrop of a dramatic new first-floor panoramic window, this performance space and demonstration stage with a working kitchen highlights Americans' quest for the new. Programming is linked to the ideas of innovation presented on the floor as well as to food, music, and theater, through which visitors can better understand American history. Daily schedules are available at americanhistory.si.edu and the information desk.

ARCHIVES CENTER

The museum's Archives Center shows highlights from its collections in changing displays.

WEST WING: THE NATION WE BUILD TOGETHER

STAR-SPANGLED BANNER GALLERY

The museum is home to the Star-Spangled Banner, the flag that inspired the national anthem. Visitors are able to view the flag in an atmosphere reminiscent of the "dawn's early light"—what Francis Scott Key experienced on the morning of September 14, 1814—and learn about its history and preservation.

WELCOME CENTER

The Nina and Ivan Selin Welcome Center, adjacent to the Mall entrance, helps visitors make the most of their time at the museum by providing easy access to information about exhibitions, tours, programs, and amenities.

GEORGE WASHINGTON STATUE
LANDMARK OBJECT – THE NATION WE BUILD TOGETHER

This marble statue of George Washington was sculpted by Horatio Greenough under commission by the US government in 1832. Designed as an allusion to Phidias's Olympian Zeus, the sculpture was originally unveiled in the Capitol Rotunda in 1841 and later moved to the Capitol's lawn. The statue came to the Smithsonian in 1908 and debuted in this building in 1964.

WITHIN THESE WALLS

"Within These Walls . . ." tells the history of a house that stood at 16 Elm Street in Ipswich, Massachusetts, and five of the many families who occupied it from the mid-1760s through 1945. The exhibition explores some of the important ways ordinary people, in their daily lives, have been part of the great changes and events in American history. The centerpiece is the largest artifact in the museum: a Georgian-style, 2 1/2–story, timber-framed house built in the 1760s, saved from the bulldozer by the citizens of Ipswich in 1963, and relocated to this space. Within this house, American colonists created new ways of living, patriots sparked a revolution, an African American struggled for freedom, community activists organized to end slavery, immigrants built new identities for themselves, and a grandmother and her grandson served on the home front during World War II.

Coming in Summer 2017:

MANY VOICES, ONE NATION

AMERICAN DEMOCRACY: THE GREAT LEAP OF FAITH

RELIGION IN AMERICA

A 2 1/2 –story timber-framed house from 1760 was brought to the museum from Ipswich, Massachusetts, in 1963 and is the centerpiece of the exhibition "Within These Walls . . ."

GREENSBORO LUNCH COUNTER
LANDMARK OBJECT – AMERICAN IDEALS

On February 1, 1960, four African American students sat down at this counter and asked to be served. They remained in their seats even though they were refused service and asked to leave. Their "passive sit-down demand" began the first sustained sit-in and ignited a youth-led movement to challenge injustice and inequality throughout the South. This defiant movement heightened many Americans' awareness of racial injustice and ultimately led to the desegregation of the F. W. Woolworth lunch counter on July 25, 1960.

ALBERT H. SMALL DOCUMENTS GALLERY

This intimate gallery allows the museum to show changing displays of fragile documents and photographs. Check the museum's Web site for current information.

AMERICAN STORIES

"American Stories" showcases historic and cultural touchstones of American history through more than 100 objects from the museum's vast holdings, including Dorothy's ruby slippers, the rarely displayed walking stick used by Benjamin Franklin, Abraham Lincoln's gold pocket watch, Muhammad Ali's boxing gloves, and a fragment of Plymouth Rock. A chronological look at the people, inventions, issues, and events that shape the American experience, "American Stories" introduces American history and provides changing exhibition space for new acquisitions.

On February 1, 1960, four African American students refused to leave the lunch counter at F. W. Woolworth's in Greensboro, North Carolina, when they were denied service. Their defiance heightened many Americans' awareness of racial injustice and ultimately led to the desegregation of the counter.

Archie Bunker's chair from "All in the Family" on display in "American Stories."

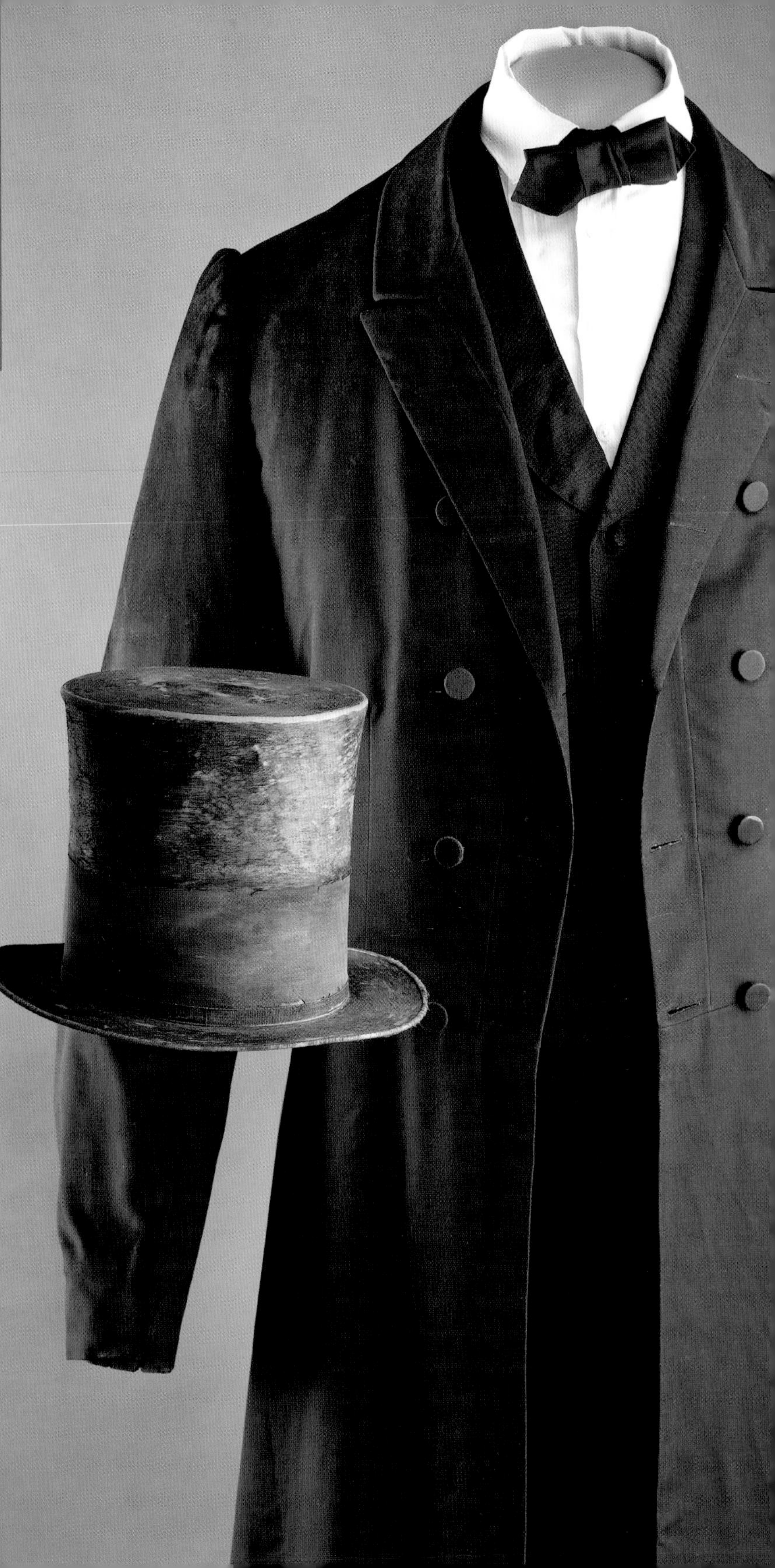

THE AMERICAN PRESIDENCY:
A GLORIOUS BURDEN

"The American Presidency: A Glorious Burden" looks at the personal, public, ceremonial, and executive actions of the men who have held this office and impacted the course of history in the past 200 years. More than 900 artifacts, including national treasures from the Smithsonian's vast presidential collections, bring to life the role of the presidency in American culture. Among the exhibition's highlights are Thomas Jefferson's wooden lap desk on which he wrote the Declaration of Independence; the carriage Ulysses S. Grant rode to his second inauguration; the top hat worn by Abraham Lincoln the night of his assassination; George Washington's battle sword; and Bill Clinton's military case used to contain the topmost national security information.

THE PRICE OF FREEDOM: AMERICANS AT WAR

This 18,000-square-foot exhibition surveys the history of the US military from the colonial era to the present, exploring ways that wars have been defining episodes in American history. Using a unique blend of more than 800 original artifacts, graphic images, and interactive stations, the exhibition tells the story of how Americans have fought to establish the nation's independence, determine its borders, shape its values of freedom and opportunity, and define its leading role in world affairs.

Among the objects included in the exhibition are one of the few Revolutionary War uniforms in existence; furniture used by General Ulysses S. Grant and Robert E. Lee during the surrender ceremony at Appomattox Court House; a restored "Huey" helicopter, an icon of the Vietnam War and the largest object on display; and the uniform Colin Powell wore during Operation Desert Storm.

Above: Uniform worn by Brigadier General Peter Gansevoort during the American Revolution. This is one of the few Revolutionary War uniforms in existence. Opposite: Abraham Lincoln wore this suit comprising a black broadcloth coat, trousers, and vest during his presidency. The hat is the one he wore to Ford's Theatre the night of his assassination. Below: Thomas Jefferson drafted the Declaration of Independence on this portable desk from 1865.

One of the famous
Vietnam-era UH-1H
"Huey" helicopters.

GUNBOAT PHILADELPHIA

In October 1776, American troops in a ragtag collection of newly built boats faced an advancing line of British ships on Lake Champlain in New York. The Americans, under the command of Benedict Arnold, were forced to retreat, but not before they fought the British to a standstill. One of the American vessels, *Philadelphia*, sank during the battle and rested on the bottom of the lake until 1935. It was recovered that year with much of its equipment intact, and came to the museum in 1964, complete with the 24-pound ball that had sent the gunboat to the bottom.

THE FIRST LADIES

"The First Ladies" explores the unofficial but important position of first lady and the ways different women have shaped the role to make contributions to the presidential administrations and the nation. The exhibition features more than two dozen gowns from the Smithsonian's almost 100-year-old First Ladies Collection, including those worn by Frances Cleveland, Lou Hoover, Jacqueline Kennedy, Laura Bush, and Michelle Obama. A section titled "Changing Times, Changing First Ladies" highlights the interests and responsibilities of Dolley Madison, Mary Lincoln, Edith Roosevelt, and Lady Bird Johnson and their achievements during their husband's administrations. "The First Ladies" encourages visitors to consider the changing roles played by the first ladies and American women over the past 200 years.

THE AMERICAN PRESIDENCY:
A GLORIOUS BURDEN

This exhibition explores the personal, public, ceremonial, and executive actions of the 44 men who have had a huge impact on the course of history in the past 200 years. More than 400 objects, including national treasures from the Smithsonian's vast presidential collections, bring to life the role of the presidency in American culture. The visitor discovers the nation's highest office through multiple thematic sections, a timeline, and media presentations.

The Continental fleet's gunboat *Philadelphia*, which sank in battle in 1776, was discovered and raised from Lake Champlain in 1935.

Antonio Stradivari (1644?–1737) of Cremona, Italy, crafted a number of decorated string instruments that are now in the museum's collection, including those known as the *Ole Bull,* a violin made in 1687, the *Greffuhle* violin from 1709, the *Axelrod* viola built in 1695, and the *Marylebone* cello of 1688.

HALL OF MUSIC

The Hall of Music is the home of the Smithsonian Chamber Music Society. Check the museum's Web site for concert schedules.

TAKING AMERICA TO LUNCH

"Taking America to Lunch" celebrates the history of American lunch boxes. After lunch boxes reached the height of their popularity at the dawn of the television era, lunch box sales became barometers for what was hip in popular culture at any point in time. Included in the display are approximately 75 objects drawn from the museum's collection of children's and workers' illustrated metal lunch boxes and beverage containers dating from the 1880s through the 1980s.

GENERAL INFORMATION

For information and maps, visit the Welcome Center on the second floor or the information desk on the first floor. Information is also available online at americanhistory.si.edu.

PUBLIC PROGRAMS, TOURS, AND DEMONSTRATIONS

The museum offers tours and public programs daily. For information about tours, concerts, lectures, living history theater, and more, inquire at the information desk or Welcome Center, call 202-633-1000, or visit the museum's Web site. For inquiries about school tours, call 202-633-3717 or visit the museum's Web site.

For generations, the lunch containers many of us hauled to school and work have reflected American culture. Of all the bags, boxes, trays, cans, and cartons we have carried over the past century, the most message-laden is the metal lunch box. A selection of boxes and their drink containers from the collections of the National Museum of American History explores this colorful heritage.

WHERE TO EAT

The Stars and Stripes Café offers a variety of all-American favorites on the lower level. In LeRoy Neiman Jazz Café on the first floor, visitors can enjoy light fare, espresso, hand-dipped ice cream, and a view onto bustling Constitution Avenue.

MUSEUM STORES

Museum stores located on the first and second floors offer a wide variety of objects and publications relating to American history, plus postcards, film, T-shirts, posters, and more.

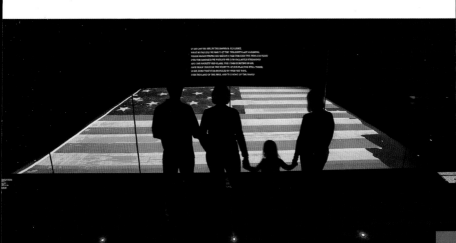

Mixtec-Aztec
Shield, 15th century.

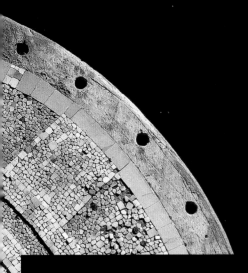

In Washington, DC:
4th Street and
Independence
Avenue, SW.
Open daily from
10 A.M. to 5:30 P.M.
Closed December 25.
Metrorail: L'Enfant
Plaza station.
Smithsonian
information:
202-633-1000

NATIONAL MUSEUM OF
THE AMERICAN INDIAN

The National Museum of the American
Indian is an institution of living cultures
dedicated to advancing knowledge and
understanding of the life, languages,
literature, history, and arts of the Native
peoples of the Americas.

The museum is housed in three
facilities: the National Museum of the
American Indian on the National Mall
in Washington, DC; the George Gustav
Heye Center in New York City; and the
Cultural Resources Center in Suitland,
Maryland (open by appointment only).

In New York City:
The George Gustav
Heye Center,
Alexander Hamilton
US Custom House,
One Bowling Green.
Open 10 A.M. to 5 P.M.;
Thursdays until 8 P.M.
Closed December 25.
212-514-3700
americanindian.si.edu

In Suitland, MD:
Cultural Resources
Center,
4220 Silver Hill Road
301-238-1435

Opposite: Shuar *Akitiai* (ear ornaments), Upper Amazon, Ecuador. Collected in 1935. Below, clockwise from lower left: Storyteller bracelet, by Joseph Coriz, Santo Domingo Pueblo, ca. 1990; Bracelet, by Angie Reano Owen, Santo Domingo Pueblo, ca. 1988; Bracelet, by Jesse Monongye (Navajo/Hopi), ca. 1983. All from Indian Arts and Crafts Board Collection, Department of the Interior, at the National Museum of the American Indian, Smithsonian Institution.

The National Museum of the American Indian (NMAI) on the National Mall opened in 2004 as a major exhibition space as well as a center for performances, films, events, and educational activities. Designed in consultation with Native people, the sweeping curvilinear building represents the spirit of Native America on the nation's front lawn and symbolizes the enduring presence of American Indians in contemporary life.

Opened in October 1994, the George Gustav Heye Center in lower Manhattan, in the heart of the financial district, serves as the National Museum of the American Indian's exhibition and education facility in New York City. Located in the Alexander Hamilton US Custom House, one of the most splendid Beaux-Arts buildings in New York, the Heye Center features permanent and temporary exhibitions, as well as a range of public programs—including music and dance performances, films, and symposia—that explore the diversity of Native peoples and the strength and continuity of their cultures from earliest times to the present. The facility also includes a resource office where visitors can learn more about Native peoples, and a Film and Video Center, which houses a collection of recent works by independent and Native American filmmakers.

The Cultural Resources Center (CRC) is home to the museum's extensive collections and serves as a research facility for Native and non-Native scholars. Located just outside Washington, DC, in Suitland,

Maryland, the CRC provides state-of-the-art resources and facilities for the conservation, handling, cataloging, and study of the museum's collections, library holdings, and photo and paper archives.

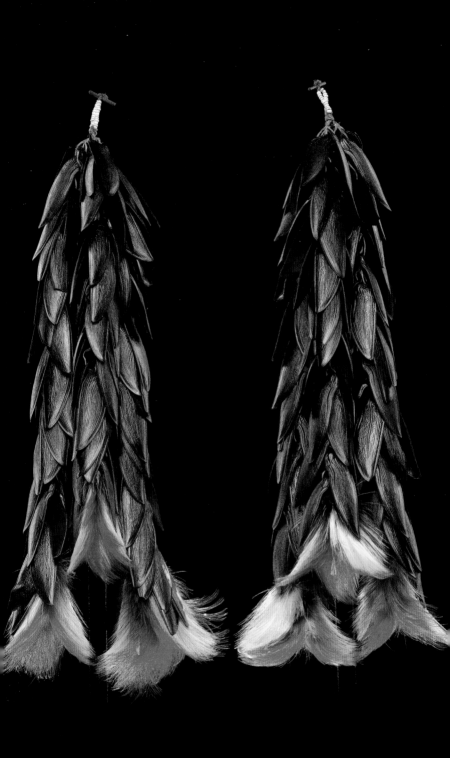

COLLECTIONS

The collections of the former Museum of the American
Indian, Heye Foundation, are the cornerstone of the
National Museum of the American Indian. Assembled
largely by wealthy New Yorker George Gustav Heye
(1874–1957), the collections span more than 10,000
years of Native heritage in the United States (including
Hawaiʻi), Canada, and Latin America. Among the thousands of masterworks are intricate wood, horn, and
stone carvings from the Northwest Coast of North
America; elegantly painted hides and garments from
the Great Plains; pottery and basketry from
the southwestern United States; ceramic figures
from the Caribbean; jade carved by the Olmec
and Maya peoples; textiles and gold offerings made
by Andean cultures; elaborate featherwork by the
peoples of Amazonia; and paintings and other
works by contemporary Native American
artists. About 70 percent of the 800,000
objects represent cultures in the United
States and Canada; 30 percent represent
cultures in Mexico and Central and
South America.

NMAI ON THE NATIONAL MALL

The museum on the National Mall was designed by
Douglas Cardinal (Blackfoot) and a team of Native architects and consultants to blend into the Mall's urban
yet park-like setting while retaining Native values.
Natural features of the land, as well as the stone and
masonry work of Chaco Canyon, Machu Picchu, and
other Native sites, inspired the museum's designers to
create a structure in which nature's rugged beauty and
architecture's creative elegance come together in perfect harmony. The five-story, 250,000-square-foot,
curvilinear building, clad in magnificent Kasota lime-
stone from Minnesota, evokes a natural rock formation
swept by wind and water. Its dome, representative of
the circular shapes in many Native cultures, complements the domed neoclassical buildings nearby.

NMAI LANDSCAPE FEATURES

- More than 40 rocks and boulders, called Grandfather Rocks— the elders of the landscape.
- Cardinal Direction Markers: four special stones placed along the north-south and east-west axes of the center of the building.
- More than 27,000 indigenous plants of 150 species.
- More than 25 native tree species, including red maple, staghorn sumac, and white oak.
- Marsh marigolds, cardinal flowers, and silky willows can be found in the wetlands.
- Buttercups, fall panic grass, black-eyed Susans, and sunflowers are featured in the meadow.
- A water feature that pays homage to Tiber Creek, which originally ran through the site.

The museum's grounds reflect the importance of Native peoples' connection to the land. The landscape presents four environments indigenous to the Chesapeake Bay region: hardwood forest, wetlands, cropland, and meadow areas. Cardinal Direction Marker stones from Maryland, Canada, Hawai'i, and Chile stand with more than 40 large, uncarved rocks and boulders called Grandfather Rocks—reminders of the longevity of Native Americans' relationship to the natural world. The landscape also includes a water feature, which begins

Northern Cardinal Direction Marker outside the National Museum of the American Indian. The Tlicho (Dogrib) community of Behchoko, in Canada's Northwest Territories, blessed the stone before its journey to Washington, DC.

AT A GLANCE

Spanning the Western Hemisphere from the Arctic Circle to Tierra del Fuego, the collections of the National Museum of the American Indian are among the finest and most comprehensive assemblages of Native cultural materials in the world. Established by an act of Congress in 1989, the museum works in collaboration with the indigenous peoples of the Western Hemisphere, including Hawai'i, to protect and foster cultures, reaffirm traditions and beliefs, encourage contemporary artistic expression, and provide a forum for Native perspectives.

as a powerful cascade tumbling over boulders at the northwest corner of the building. The water continues to flow beside the entry path, ending in a quiet pool beside the museum's main entrance.

The entrance to the National Museum of the American Indian on the National Mall faces east toward the rising sun. Just beyond the entrance extends the Potomac Atrium, a circular gathering place for music, dance, cultural events, and tours. The Potomac—from an Algonquian-Powhatan word meaning "where the goods are brought in"—features a 120-foot-high atrium and eight large prism windows that, on sunny days, project a palette of brilliant rainbow colors throughout the space. *Eagle and the Young Chief,* a 22-foot cedar totem pole created by Tsimshian artist David A. Boxley (b. 1952) and his son, David R. Boxley (b. 1981), weighs 2,500 pounds and welcomes visitors into the Potomac Atrium.

The museum has several locations for Native presentations, drama, dance, music performances, demonstrations, readings, panel discussions, and seminars, including the 300-seat Rasmuson Theater (1st level). The Lelawi Theater (4th level) presents *Who We Are,* a 13-minute film that celebrates the vitality and diversity of Native life.

Exhibitions on the second, third, and fourth levels can be accessed from elevators located in the Potomac

space. At the imagiNATIONS Activity Center (3rd level), visitors, especially those ages 5 through 12, will find this interactive, family-friendly space filled with a multitude of unique learning experiences.

The Mitsitam Native Foods Cafe (1st level) serves meals and snacks based on the indigenous foods of the Americas.

The Chesapeake Museum Store (1st level) features jewelry, textiles, and other works by Native artisans.

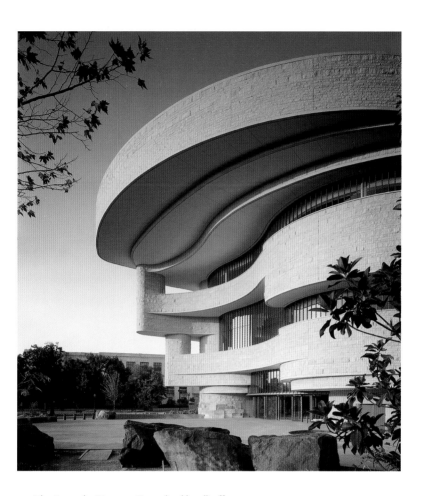

The Roanoke Museum Store (2nd level) offers a wide variety of merchandise, including books, crafts, music, souvenirs, and toys.

EXHIBITIONS

The National Museum of the American Indian on the National Mall presents diverse exhibitions, ranging from explorations of historical materials from the museum's vast collections to exhibitions of contemporary Native artistic expressions. Permanent exhibitions include "Our Universes: Traditional Knowledge Shapes Our World" (4th level); "Return to a Native Place: Algonquian Peoples of the Chesapeake" (2nd level); and an introductory display near the museum's

Above: East-facing entrance of the National Museum of the American Indian on the National Mall. Opposite: Klikitat Yakama Nation beaded bag, late 1800s.

Raven Steals Sun
by Preston Singletary
(Tlingit, b. 1963),
Seattle, Washington,
2003, blown and
sand-carved glass.

entrance that provides an overview of Native community, expression, encounter, and innovation. "Window on Collections: Many Hands, Many Voices" (3rd and 4th levels) showcases Native-made dolls, beadwork, containers, animals, games, and other objects.

The Sealaska Gallery (2nd level) will showcase a series of smaller exhibitions based on the museum's collections as well as changing contemporary exhibitions.

Treaties lie at the heart of the relationship between Indian Nations and the United States. "Nation to Nation: Treaties Between the United States and American Indian Nations," the story of that relation-

Hattie Tom (Chiricahua, Apache), Omaha, Nebraska, ca. 1899.

ship, covers the history and legacy of United States–American Indian diplomacy from the colonial period through the present.

Exhibitions at the George Gustav Heye Center in New York City will include "Circle of Dance," which presents Native dance as a vibrant, meaningful, and diverse form of cultural expression. Featuring ten social and ceremonial dances from throughout the Americas, the exhibition illuminates the significance of each dance and the unique characteristics of its movements and music. Also in New York City is "Infinity of Nations: History and Art in the Collections of the National Museum of the American Indian," a major exhibition that showcases the cultural, historical, and geographic scope of the museum's holdings.

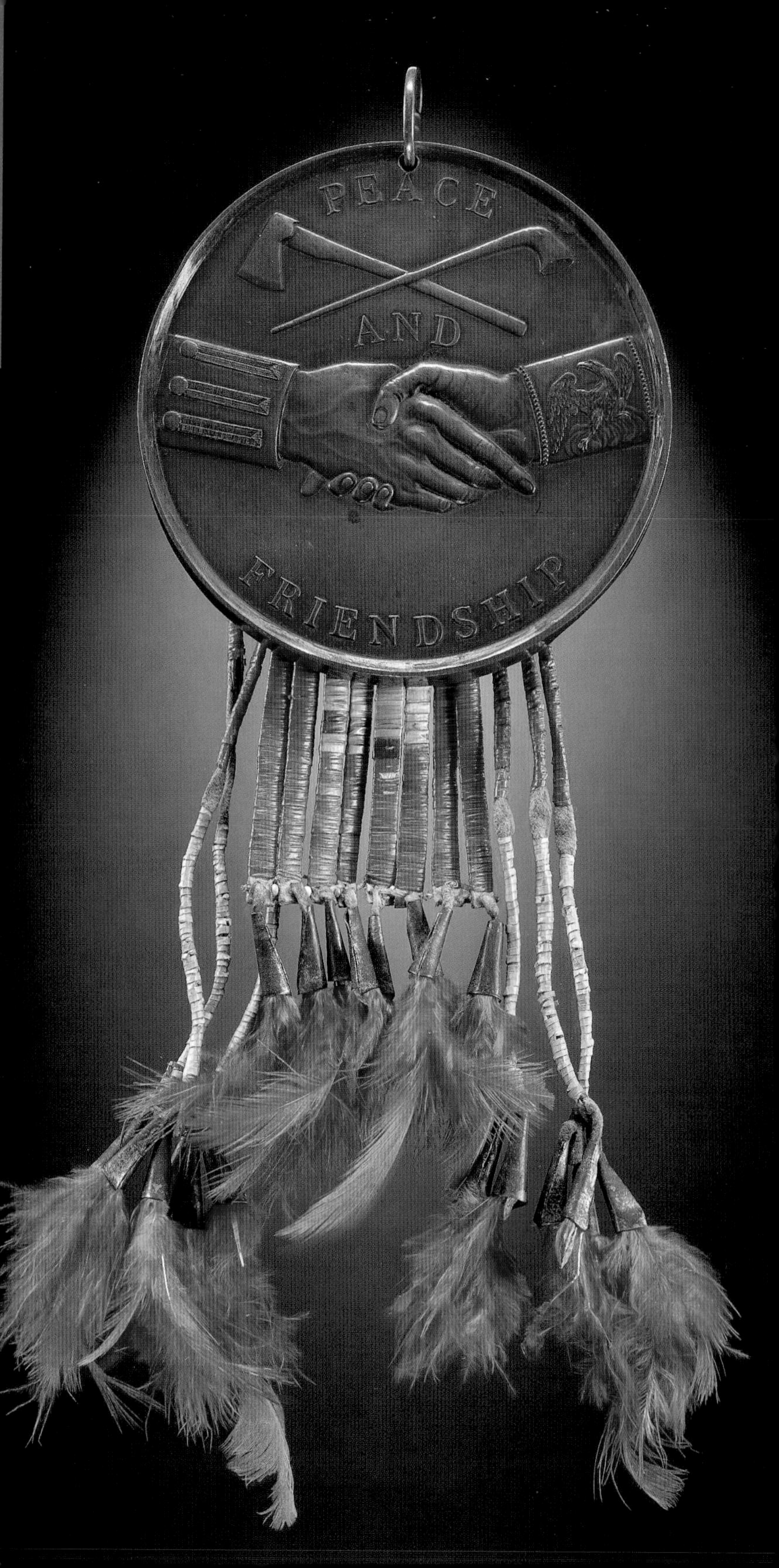
PEACE
AND
FRIENDSHIP

of the museum's educational programs, visit our Web site at americanindian.si.edu/education.

PUBLIC PROGRAMS

The National Museum of the American Indian provides opportunities for museum visitors to experience the living arts, cultures, and lifeways of the indigenous peoples of the Western Hemisphere and Hawai'i through performances, demonstrations, workshops, and the spoken word. For more information, e-mail the Cultural Arts staff at NMAIprograms@si.edu or visit our Web site at americanindian.si.edu for a calendar of events.

MEMBERSHIP

To become an NMAI member and receive its full-color quarterly magazine *American Indian,* call 800-242-NMAI (6624) or click on Membership and Giving on the Web site.

RESOURCE CENTERS

The National Museum of the American Indian has a Resource Center at the George Gustav Heye Center in New York City. In the open "library" areas, visitors can ask questions, explore DVDs, CD-ROMs, and Web sites, watch movies, handle objects, or research areas of interest. The center has a reference

GENERAL INFORMATION
INFORMATION DESKS

The National Museum of the American Indian, Washington, DC: Visitor and membership information can be obtained at the Welcome Desk on the first level. Daily program information is also posted throughout the museum.

The George Gustav Heye Center, New York: The information desk is located in the Great Hall, on the second floor across from the main museum entrance.

EDUCATIONAL PROGRAMS

A variety of interactive tours as well as special cultural presentations and films are offered for school groups. Reservations for these popular programs are required and should be made well in advance. To arrange a school group tour or program at the Mall museum, call 202-633-6644 or 1-888-618-0572, or e-mail NMAI-Group-Reservations@si.edu. To arrange school group programs at the Heye Center, call 212-514-3705. For information about the full range

Above left: Maya polychrome vase, Nebaj, Guatemala, A.D. 550–850. Opposite: Thomas Jefferson peace medal, 1801, owned by Powder Face (Northern Inunaina/Arapaho), Oklahoma, bronze copper alloy, hide, porcupine quills, feathers, dye, and metal cones

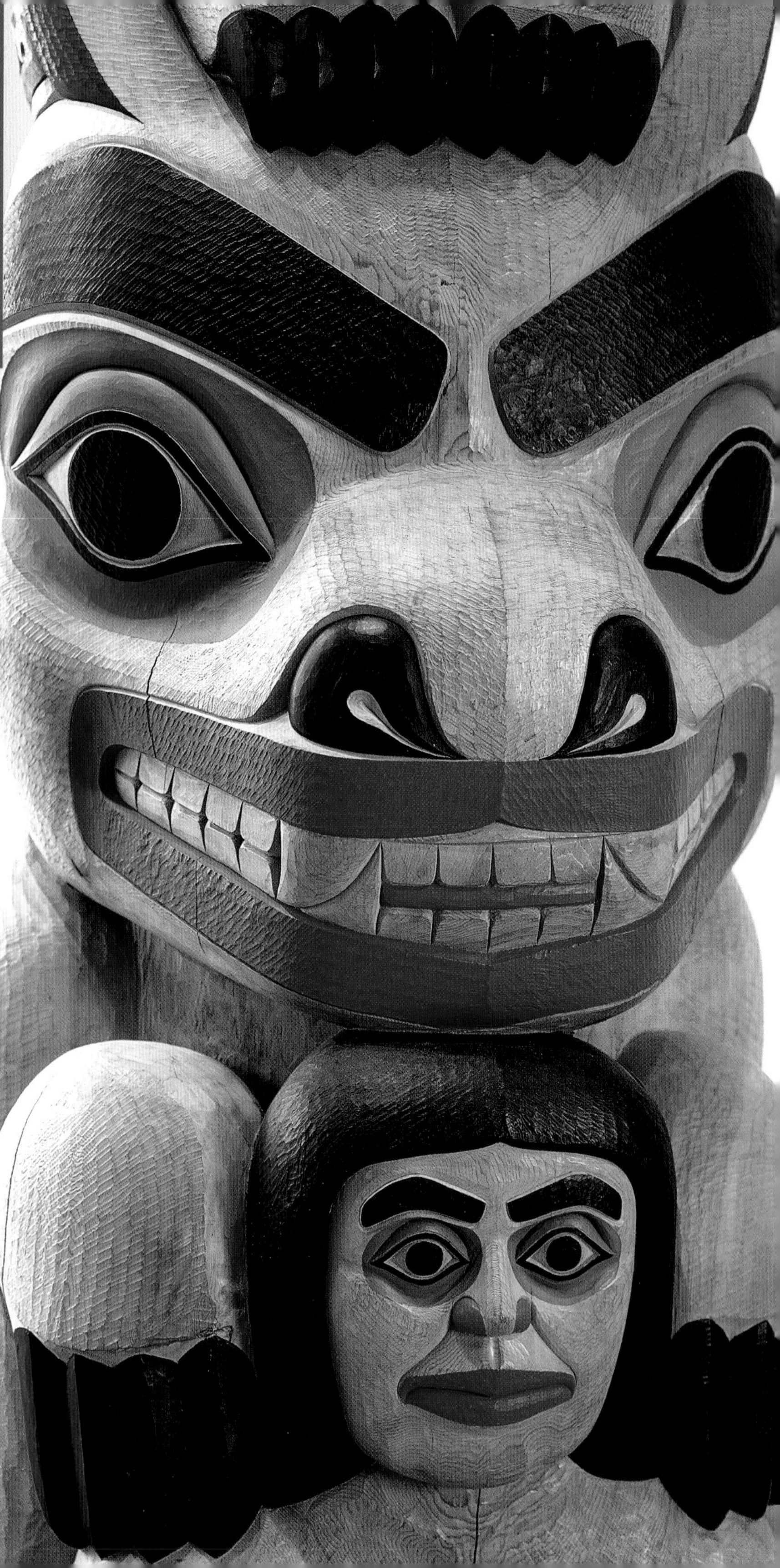

desk, study area, videos, hands-on collection boxes, and an Interactive Learning Center, all of which are open to the public during museum hours.

Appointments can also be made to use the Heye Center's Haudenosaunee Discovery Room, a hands-on learning center for children. For information about Resource Center programs at the Heye Center, call 212-514-3799.

FILM AND VIDEO

The Film and Video Center of the National Museum of the American Indian offers public presentations and information services about films, video, radio, television, and new media produced by and about the indigenous peoples of the Western Hemisphere. It organizes the NMAI's biennial Native American Film and Video Festival and screenings at the museum and in venues across the country. For information about film and video at the National Museum of the American Indian in Washington, DC, call 202-633-6694. For information about film and video at the Heye Center, call 212-514-3737.

MUSEUM AND GALLERY SHOPS

The National Museum of the American Indian in Washington, DC, has two stores. The Chesapeake Museum Store, on the museum's first level, features jewelry, textiles, and other works by Native artisans. The Roanoke Museum Store, on the museum's second level, carries souvenirs and children's books and toys.

The Heye Center in New York has two stores. The Gallery Shop, featuring books and unique, handmade Indian jewelry and textiles, is located on the second floor near the main entrance. The Museum Store, with gifts, books, and toys related to Native American culture, is on the first floor.

MITSITAM NATIVE FOODS CAFE

The Mall museum's Zagat-rated café offers entrees, side dishes, snacks, desserts, and beverages based on the culinary traditions of five geographic regions covering the entire Western Hemisphere: Northern Woodlands, South America, Northwest Coast, Great Plains, and Mesoamerica. Named "Mitsitam," meaning "let's eat" in the Piscataway and Delaware languages, the popular cafe is the first museum dining facility to cover a broad spectrum of Native foods and cultures.

Located on the musem's first level, across from the Rasmuson Theater, the Mitsitam Native Foods Cafe is open daily from 11 A.M. to 5 P.M. The full menu is available from 11 A.M. to 3 P.M., with a smaller menu available from 3 P.M. to 5 P.M.

Opposite: *Kaats* (detail), 2004. Carved by Nathan P. Jackson (Tlingit) and Stephen P. Jackson (Tlingit); painted by Dorica R. Jackson.

Above: Lieutenant Henry Samuel Hawker R.N., *The Portuguese slaver Diligenté captured by H. M. Sloop Pearl with 600 slaves on board, taken in charge to Nassau May 1838* (detail), 1838, watercolor on paper. **Opposite:** Vest worn by Jimi Hendrix, 1960s. Velvet, braid, plastic, and metal.

NATIONAL MUSEUM OF AFRICAN AMERICAN HISTORY AND CULTURE

The National Museum of African American History and Culture (NMAAHC) was established by an act of Congress in 2003 that made it the 19th museum of the Smithsonian Institution. The museum is a place where all Americans can learn about the richness and diversity of the African American experience, what it means to their lives, and how it helped shape this nation. Scheduled for completion in the fall of 2016, it sits on five acres on Constitution Avenue between 14th and 15th Streets, NW.

During the construction phase, the museum has produced publications, hosted public programs, and built its collections. It has also presented exhibitions at museums across the country and in its own gallery on the second floor of the Smithsonian's National Museum of American History.

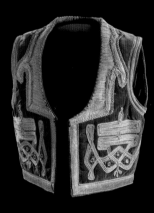

Opposite: Tuskegee Airman flight jacket worn by Lieutenant Colonel Woodrow W. Crockett, 1942. Manufactured by Aero Leather Clothing Co. Leather, cloth, metal, paint. Gift of Lt. Col. Woodrow W. Crockett.

Railroad passenger car from the Jim Crow era, Southern Railway No. 1200, 1922. Steel and glass. Pullman Palace Car Co. Gift of Pete Claussen and Gulf and Ohio Railways.

A PLACE FOR US ALL

The National Museum of African American History and Culture (NMAAHC) presents a view of America through the lens of African American history and culture in a setting that transcends the boundaries of race and culture. The museum focuses on the story that unites us all. Exhibitions have been conceived to help transform visitors' understanding of American history and culture and adapt to and participate in changing definitions of American citizenship, liberty, and equality. Exhibitions employ a range of interpretive and experiential strategies in exploring three major themes: history, culture, and community. An array of interactive programs and educational resources is available on the museum's Web site, nmaahc.si.edu.

THE BUILDING

The architecture of the museum is derived from the classical tripartite column (base, shaft, and capital). In Yoruban art and architecture, the column, or wooden post, is traditionally crafted with a three-tiered capital. This corona form is the central idea behind the design

of the museum: reaching toward the sky, it expresses faith, hope, and resiliency. Inside, a series of windows frame specific views of the city. The framed perspectives remind us that the museum presents a view of America as seen through the lens of African American history and culture.

HISTORY

Three of the four public floors belowground house the History galleries.

The "Slavery and Freedom" exhibition tells a story not only of people but also of an economic engine that transformed America. It illustrates the inextricable link between freedom and enslavement in America, up to the Reconstruction.

"Defending Freedom, Defining Freedom: Era of Segregation 1966–1968" focuses on the period from post-Reconstruction through the aftermath of the Civil Rights Act of 1968. It looks closely at the various permutations of tragic violence fundamental to segregation.

Above: Boxing headgear worn by Muhammad Ali, ca. 1973. Created by Everlast Worldwide, Inc. Leather, padding, cloth, and metal.

Boombox carried by Radio Raheem in the film *Do the Right Thing*, 1989. Manufactured by Tecsonic, signed by Spike Lee, owned by Gene Siskel. Plastic, metal, wire, cloth, pressure-sensitive tape, and ink.

"A Changing America: 1968 and Beyond" is an exhibition that continues the historical chronology to the present and prompts visitors to think about how their lives are affected by the African American struggle for freedom and how it might inspire them to action.

CULTURE

Aboveground, two floors (3rd and 4th) showcase the Community and Culture galleries.

The large "Musical Crossroads" exhibition promises to be an exciting, dynamic investigation and celebration of African American music. Part show, part interactive, and part exhibit, the gallery looks at music's vital role in freedom struggles—from the plantation to civil rights marches, from the dance floor and recording studio to the airwaves—in a way that will have visitors tuning in and even dancing. The gallery provides an opportunity for audiences to explore the entire African American experience.

The "Cultural Expressions" exhibition marks the contributions of African Americans in cultural expressions including fashion, food, artistry, and language.

The Visual Arts Gallery showcases a portion of the museum's permanent collection of visual arts, which includes paintings, sculptures, and works on paper. The gallery provides a changing space for exhibitions of work in all mediums.

The Earl W. and Amanda Stafford Center for African American Media Arts on the second floor presents a rotating display of imagery from the museum's one-of-a-kind photography and visual media collection and affords visitors the means to explore the collection digitally.

TAKING THE STAGE

This exhibition explores the history of African Americans in theater, film, and television to celebrate their creative achievements, demonstrate their cultural impact, and illuminate their struggles for equal representation on the stage of American entertainment. Visitors see how African Americans transformed the ways they are represented onstage by challenging racial discrimination and stereotypes and striving to produce more positive, authentic, and diverse images of African American identity and experience. Together these stories suggest how African American performing artists also paved the way for broader social change. Stories include Paul Robeson's role in *Othello*, Ntozake Shange's *For Colored Girls Who Have Considered Suicide/When the Rainbow Is Enuf*, and the Black Stuntmen's Assocation in Hollywood.

COMMUNITY

The "Power of Place" exhibition interprets the range of African American experiences in the country by looking at regionalism. Visitors are able to investigate different places and eras at a time. The gallery emphasizes that the African American experience is not just one story—but is a composite of stories from across the nation.

The Sports Gallery celebrates how African Americans have changed sports in our nation, and it delves into the role sports has played in helping people survive and change life in America.

MAKING A WAY OUT OF NO WAY

The stories in this exhibition show the ways in which African Americans created possibilities in a world that denied them opportunities. The stories reflect the perseverance, resourcefulness, and resilience required by African Americans to survive and thrive in America.

Poster for Mattie Wilkes performance at Holliday Street Theater, 1899-1905. Produced by H. C. Miner Lithographing Company. Ink on paper.

The Mothership, 1990s reconstruction after 1970s original. Designed by Jules Fisher and George Clinton; used by Parliament-Funkadelic. Metal, plastic, glass. Gift of Love to the Planet.

French Croix de Guerre
medal received by
Lawrence McVey, 369th
Infantry Regiment, United
States Army, 1918.
Issued by French
Republic, designed by
Paul-Albert Bartholome.
Bronze and ribbon.

NAACP Spingarn Medal
awarded to Major
Charles Young, 1916.
Created by National As-
sociation for the Ad-
vancement of Colored
People, issued by Joel
Elias Spingarn. Gold.

MILITARY HISTORY GALLERY

The military gallery exhibition conveys a sense of appreciation and respect for the military service of
African Americans from the American Revolution to
the current war on terrorism. It establishes an understanding that the African American military experience
shapes opportunities for the greater community and
has profoundly shaped the nation. The exhibition helps
visitors understand the African American military experience in three areas: "Struggle for Freedom" focusing on the American Revolution, the War of 1812, and
the Civil War; "Segregated Military," about the Indian
Wars, Spanish-American War, and World Wars I and II;
and "Stirrings of Change to a Colorblind Military," ex-
amining the Korean and Vietnam wars and today's war
on terrorism. Artifacts include Civil War badges,
weapons, and photographs, Flag of the 9th Regiment
US Colored Volunteers, a World War I Croix de Guerre
medal awarded to US soldier Lawrence McVey, and
various Tuskegee Airmen materials.

CENTRAL HALL

The grand central hall, the main entrance of the
museum on Constitution Avenue, welcomes visitors,
creates a sense of awe, and awakens visitors to the
museum experience.

SUPPLEMENTAL GALLERIES

The Youth Gallery accommodates children of all ages
and their families. Here, presentations address and
interpret the same major themes explored throughout
the museum but in ways that especially engage a young
audience. The Youth Gallery encourages all visitors to
think about who they are and how they can make a
difference.

The Changing Gallery accommodates dynamic traveling shows.

GET INVOLVED

Excitement continues to grow around the creation of
the new National Museum of African American History

and Culture. We have a lot to accomplish. If you have the time, interest, and energy to help, check out opportunities to do so at nmaahc.si.edu.

GENERAL INFORMATION

Located at the corner of 15th Street N.W. and Constitution Avenue, the museum includes exhibition galleries, an education center, theater, auditorium, café, store and offices. Visitors will enter the museum through the grand Porch at south (National Mall) side of the building, while a secondary entrance is provided on the north (Constitution Avenue) side.

Costume gown for Glinda the Good Witch in *The Wiz: The Super Soul Musical "Wonderful Wizard of Oz,"* worn by Dee Dee Bridgewater, 1975. Designed by Geoffrey Holder, created by Grace Costumes Inc. Synthetic fiber and chiffon. Gift of the Black Fashion Museum founded by Lois K. Alexander-Lane.

As visitors move through the exhibitions, a series of openings frame views of the Washington Monument, the White House and other Smithsonian museums along the Mall. These openings or "lenses" offer respite and pause at selected moments along the exhibition experience. The framed perspectives serve as a reminder that the museum presents a view of America through the lens of African American history and culture.

The Contemplative Court provides a water-and light-filled memorial area that offers visitors a quiet space for reflection. A raised overhead oculus (circular window) allows light to enter the space.

One of the largest spaces in the museum, the 350-seat Oprah Winfrey Theater will be a forum in the nation's capital for performers, artists, educators, scholars, authors, musicians, filmmakers and opinion leaders. The theater's programs will enable audiences to gain a broader understanding of how African American history and culture shape and enrich the country and the world.

Above: Detail of part of a frieze carved in high relief. Pakistan or Afghanistan, ancient Gandhara, Kushan dynasty, late 2nd–early 3rd century CE; schist. Opposite: Lidded box with figures in a landscape. China, Ming dynasty, Yongle reign, 1403–24, carved red lacquer on

FREER GALLERY OF ART

When the Freer Gallery of Art opened in 1923, it was the Smithsonian's first fine art museum and one of the first museums in the world devoted to Asian art. Its internationally preeminent collection of art includes works produced over six millennia throughout the Asian continent, from China, Japan, Korea, and Southeast Asia to India, Iran, and the Islamic world. Exceptional examples of Neolithic Chinese jades and bronzes, ancient Egyptian art, and early biblical manuscripts are also part of the Freer's collection. In addition, the museum boasts one of the world's largest and most important group of works by American artist James McNeill Whistler, including the renowned Peacock Room. Paintings by American artists of the late 19th and early 20th century, such as

Independence Avenue (accessible entrance) at 12th Street, SW. Mall entrance: Jefferson Drive at 12th Street, SW. Open daily from 10 a.m. to 5:30 p.m. Closed December 25. Note: The Freer Gallery will be undergoing renovation until summer 2017; museum exhibitions and events will continue in the adjacent Sackler Gallery and venues around Washington. Check the museum's Web site to learn more and plan your trip. Metrorail: Smithsonian station. Smithsonian information: 202-633-1000 asia.si.edu

AT A GLANCE

The Freer Gallery of Art, complemented by the adjacent Arthur M. Sackler Gallery, houses one of the world's finest collections of Asian art. These magnificent holdings, which span Neolithic times to the early 20th century, share exhibition space in the Italian Renaissance–style building with a major group of 19th- and early 20th-century American artists. The Freer Gallery also contains the world's most comprehensive collection of works by James McNeill Whistler, including the glimmering Peacock Room, a sumptuously painted interior permanently on view.

Thomas Wilmer Dewing, John Singer Sargent, Abbott Handerson Thayer, and Dwight William Tryon, are also part of the permanent collection.

Charles Lang Freer (1854–1919), an industrialist from Detroit, Michigan, offered his personal collection of Asian and American art to the Smithsonian Institution, and his gift was accepted in 1906. Over the next 13 years, Freer's collection grew substantially, and he worked with architect Charles Adams Platt to design the Italianate structure that would house his gift to the nation. Today, the Freer Gallery of Art preserves and conveys the aesthetic vision of its founder in the uncommon presentation of Asian and American art and culture. Freer began collecting American art in the 1880s. He limited his acquisitions to the work of a few living artists and concentrated

especially on Whistler. Freer began collecting Asian art in 1887, and by the time of his death in 1919 he had assembled an unparalleled collection of Asian masterpieces. Freer once wrote that he attempted to "gather together objects of art covering various periods of production, all of which are harmonious and allied in many ways." In his bequest to the nation, Freer gave 9,000 Asian paintings, sculptures, and drawings as well as works of calligraphy, metal, lacquer, and jade. Many other generous donors have since participated in the growth of the collection, which now numbers some 26,000 objects.

Freer also donated the funds for building the museum in the Italian Renaissance style, which he believed would provide an appropriate setting for the display of his art. The loggias that surround the gracious courtyard and fountain welcome visitors to relax and enjoy the beautiful works of art on view. Today, the building is on the National Register of Historic Places and is a favored destination for those wishing to escape the bustle of the city.

Above: Detail of the Peacock Room, formerly a London dining room that Whistler controversially redesigned and Freer installed in his Detroit mansion before it became part of the Freer Gallery of Art. Opposite top: Whistler's *Variations in Flesh Colour and Green: The Balcony*, 1864–70, oil on wood panel. Opposite bottom: Jar, Korea, Chosen period, Yi dynasty, ca. 1900, glazed porcelain clay.

Above: *Vihagra Raga-Putra, Son of Sri Raga* from a *Ragamala,* ca. 1690, Basohli, Jammu and Kashmir, Punjab Hills, India, opaque watercolor and silver on paper.
Right: Den Shiru (1743–1805), *Geomantic Verdit from the I-Ching,* hanging scroll, ink on paper.
Opposite: The courtyard, Freer Gallery of Art.

Works from the Freer's permanent collection are frequently put on display in an ongoing program of exhibition rotations. Japanese ceramics, screens, and hanging scrolls; ancient Chinese jades and bronzes; Buddhist art; South Asian sculpture; and Islamic arts of the book are featured in the skylighted galleries. A wide range of free public concerts, films, lectures, tours, and other programs complement the works on view.

GENERAL INFORMATION

ENTRANCES

The main visitors' entrance is located on Jefferson Drive, SW. The street-level entrance on Independence Avenue has elevator service to the galleries. The Arthur M. Sackler Gallery is accessible through an underground gallery.

INFORMATION DESK

Located in the lobby near the National Mall entrance, the information desk is staffed by volunteers from 10 A.M. to 5 P.M daily.

TOURS

Free guided tours are offered daily, except Wednesdays and federal holidays. Group tours are available with four weeks' advance registration. For more information, visit asia.si.edu/tour; to schedule a tour, e-mail asiatours@si.edu.

LIBRARY

A Smithsonian library serving the Freer and Sackler Galleries is located in the Sackler. It has 60,000 to 80,000 volumes, about half of which are in Chinese and Japanese, and subscribes to more than 400 periodicals. Library hours are 10 A.M. to 5 P.M., Monday through Friday, except federal holidays.

ARCHIVES

Researchers may examine the more than 100,000 historical documents and photographic images in the archives, located in the Sackler. The Archives is open by appointment Tuesday through Thursday, 10 A.M. to 5 P.M. For an appointment, call 202-633-0533.

OPEN F|S DIGITAL COLLECTION

The full and incredibly rich collections of the Freer and Sackler Galleries—more than 40,000 objects—are available online at open.asia.si.edu for search, download, and discovery.

FILMS AND PERFORMANCES

The Freer's Meyer Auditorium hosts free concerts and films year-round, presenting both new works and beloved classics. For a full schedule, visit asia.si.edu/events.

Above: Folio from a *Falnama* (Book of omens): recto, Prophet Muhammad's night journey (Mi'raj); verso, text. Qazvin, Iran, Safavid period (1501–1722), opaque watercolor, ink, and gold on paper. Opposite top: Bell *(yong zhong)* from a set of six graduated bells, China, Eastern Zhou dynasty (770–221 BCE), bronze.

1050 Independence
Avenue, SW.
Entered from Enid A.
Haupt Garden through
ground-level pavilion.
Open daily from
10 A.M. to 5:30 P.M.
Closed December 25.
Metrorail:
Smithsonian station.
Smithsonian
information:
202-633-1000
asia.si.edu

ARTHUR M. SACKLER
GALLERY

In 1987, Dr. Arthur M. Sackler (1913–1987)
founded the museum that now bears his
name with his gift of more than a thou-
sand works of Asian art. Asia's distinctive
artistic and cultural traditions are featured
in exhibitions based on the museum's permanent collection and on those presented
by other leading collections and institutions around the world. An active program
on contemporary art explores the photography, video, film, installation art, ceramics, sculpture, and other forms of art that
are being produced in Asia today. Other
exhibitions examine art produced centuries in the past, such as the *Shahnama*,
Iran's national epic written by the poet Fir-
dawsi more than a millennium ago, or
Japanese tales of the terrifying monster

Album page, *The Angel of Death Descends on Shaddad ibn Ad.* Iran, Qazvin, Safavid period, mid-1550s–early 1560s, opaque watercolor and gold on paper.

The Sackler Gallery possesses one of the world's largest collections of works by the renowned Japanese artist Hokusai, and its collections are rich in Japanese woodblock prints and examples of manga. The collection also includes ornately decorated manuscripts and detailed portraits created in Mughal India. Galleries are devoted to innovative displays of the permanent collection, including works from China, India, Japan, Southeast Asia, and the Himalayas, and to major interna-

tional exhibitions that bring the best in Asian art and culture to Washington. Members of local Asian communities often help craft the gallery's vibrant public programs, and regular lectures bring renowned experts from around the world.

Above: Xu Bing (b. 1955), *Monkeys Grasp for the Moon,* China, 2004, lacquer on Baltic birchwood. Left: Rhyton, Iran, Sasanian period, CE 300–400, silver and gilt.

AT A GLANCE

The Arthur M. Sackler Gallery, together with the connected Freer Gallery of Art, contains one of the world's finest collections of Asian art. In addition to innovative presentations from the permanent collection, the Sackler features exciting traveling international exhibitions that display exceptional art from Japan, China, Southeast Asia, India, and the Islamic world, ranging from the ancient to the contemporary.

The Sackler Gallery involves families through its popular "ImaginAsia," a weekend program offering hands-on activities that encourage families to explore an exhibition and create a related project to take home. The workshops begin in the classroom on the second level. For more information and a full schedule, visit asia.si.edu.

Top: Shindo Susumu (b. 1952), bowl, Japan, 1992, porcelain with blue enamel glaze. Bottom: Two-headed bust, Jordan, ca. 6500 BCE, plaster and bitumen; lent by the Department of Antiquities of Jordan. Opposite: Woman's robe *(munisak)*, Central Asia, 1850–75, silk and velvet.

GENERAL INFORMATION

ENTRANCE

Enter from Independence Avenue through a ground-level pavilion and proceed to exhibition areas on three lower levels. The Freer Gallery of Art, with related exhibitions and programs, is accessible by an underground gallery.

INFORMATION DESK

Located in the entrance pavilion, information desks are staffed by volunteers from 10 A.M. to 5 P.M. daily.

TOURS

Free guided tours are offered daily, except Wednesdays and federal holidays. Group tours are available with four weeks' advance registration. For more information, visit asia.si.edu/tour; to schedule a tour, e–mail asiatours@si.edu.

GALLERY SHOP

The shop, located on the first level, features a carefully curated selection of gifts and keepsakes inspired by the museum's collections and Asian cultures. Items include porcelain, crafts, jewelry, textiles, books, prints, and cards.

LIBRARY

A Smithsonian Library serving the Freer and Sackler Galleries is located in the Sackler. The most comprehensive Asian art resource in the United States, the library contains more than 80,000 volumes and regular periodicals. Library hours are 10 A.M. to 5 P.M., Monday through Friday, except federal holidays. Visit asia.si.edu/research/library for more information or to search the online catalog.

ARCHIVES

Researchers may examine the more than 100,000 historical documents and photographic images in the archives, located in the Sackler. The Archives is open by appointment; visit asia.si.edu/research/archives for more information or to request an appointment.

Victor Ekpuk (b. 1964), Nigeria. *Composition #3,* 2009. Graphite and pastel on paper. Gift of the artist and museum purchase. Opposite top: Kota artist, Gabon. Reliquary guardian figure, late 19th–early 20th century. Wood, copper alloys, iron, and bone. Gift of Walt Disney World Co., a subsidiary of The Walt Disney Company.

NATIONAL MUSEUM OF AFRICAN ART

Founded in 1964 by Warren M. Robbins (1923–2008) to promote cross-cultural understanding through programs in the arts and social sciences, the National Museum of African Art is the nation's only museum dedicated to the collection, exhibition, conservation, and study of the arts of Africa and its diasporas. It became part of the Smithsonian Institution in 1979. The museum's collection of over 12,000 artworks is diverse in terms of time period, geography, and media.

Through its dynamic exhibitions, community outreach, and international collaborations, the National Museum of African Art seeks to inspire conversations about the beauty, power, and diversity of African arts and cultures worldwide.

950 Independence Avenue, SW.
Entered from Enid A. Haupt Garden through ground-level pavilion.
Open daily from 10 A.M. to 5:30 P.M.

Elisofon Photographic Archives (202-633-4690) and Robbins Library (202-633-4680) open weekdays by appointment.
Closed December 25.
Metrorail: Smithsonian station.
Smithsonian information:
202-633-4690
africa.si.edu

Right: Face mask, Chowke peoples, Democratic Republic of the Congo, early 20th century. Below: Bullom or Temne artist, Sapi-Portuguese style, Sierra Leone. Hunting horn, late 15th century. Ivory and metal. Gift of Walt Disney World Co., a subsidiary of The Walt Disney Company. Opposite top: Yinka Shonibare MBE (b. 1962), England. 19th Century Kid (Queen Victoria), 1999. Cloth, synthetic fiber, dyes, wood, metal, leather. Purchased with funds given in memory of Philip L. Ravenhill, the Sylvia H. Williams Memorial Fund for Acquisitions, Frieda B. Rosenthal, Barbara Croissant and Mark E. Baker. Opposite bottom: Mohammed Ahmed Abdalla (b. 1935), Sudan. Vase, 1990. Porcelainous stoneware. Purchased with funds provided by the Smithsonian Collections Acquisition Program.

COLLECTIONS

The National Museum of African Art's exhibitions present the finest examples of art from across the African continent in a wide range of mediums, spanning from 13th-century ceramics to 21st-century time-based media.

In 2005, the museum acquired the Walt Disney–Tishman African Art Collection, which contains some of the most iconic works of African art. The museum is committed to the ongoing conservation, research, and display of this world-famous collection. The museum also boasts the largest collection of contemporary African art in the United States and, since 1966, has been actively acquiring the work of some of the world's best-known artists, including El Anatsui, Sammy Baloji, William Kentridge, Julie Mehretu, and Lynette Yiadom-Boakye. The museum commissions works, including the first-ever land art exhibition installed on the National Mall.

DISCOVER!

The National Museum of African Art's public programs highlight the visual arts of Africa as a catalyst to inter-disciplinary teaching and learning, and actively promote a deeper understanding of Africa's rich artistic heritage and cultures. This is exemplified by the museum's Teen Ambassadors program, which empowers the next generation of arts leaders with in-gallery training. Teenagers become storytellers, connecting with visitors and providing outreach to local community groups.

Film screenings, guided tours, music and dance programs, scholarly symposia, workshops, and a family-friendly Discovery Room are among the free offerings to the public. Visit africa.si.edu/events for a complete schedule. Audiovisual loan programs, the collections database, downloadable lesson plans and curriculum guides, online exhibitions, and video conference distance learning expand the museum's mission beyond its walls and connect visitors with Africa and the world.

AT A GLANCE

Home to the nation's collection of African art, the National Museum of African Art celebrates the rich visual traditions and the diverse cultures of Africa and its diasporas, from ancient to contemporary times. It fosters an appreciation of African art and civilizations through the collections, exhibitions, research, and public programs. The museum, located on the National Mall, houses its collections, galleries, education facilities, conservation laboratory, research library, and photographic archives.

Right: Nontsikelelo "Lolo" Veleko (b. 1977), South Africa. *Kepi in Bree Street;* from the Beauty Is in the Eye of the Beholder series, 2006. Digital print with pigment dyes on cotton paper. Purchased with funds provided by the Annie Laurie Aitken Endowment. Below: Bamum artist, Cameroon. Male figure, late 19th century. Wood, brass, cloth, glass beads, cowrie shells. Gift of Evelyn A.J. Hall and John A. Friede.

RESEARCH FACILITIES

The National Museum of African Art is a leading research and reference center for the arts of Africa. The state-of-the-art conservation laboratory houses an x-radiography system with digital imaging and serves as an international authority on conserving African art, often collaborating with other institutions to analyze African art materials and resolve treatment problems. The Eliot Elisofon Photographic Archives (EEPA), with 350,000 prints and transparencies, extensive unedited footage, and documentary films, specializes in the collection and preservation of visual materials on Africa's arts, cultures, and environments. The Warren M. Robbins Library contains more than 50,000 volumes on African art and material culture. The museum continues to advance the field through a robust fellowship program for academics, artists, and conservators.

GENERAL INFORMATION

Stella Osarhiere
Gbinigie, Benin City,
Nigeria. Hand-colored
photograph by Solomon
Osagie Alonge, c. 1950.
Chief S.O. Alonge
Collection.

INFORMATION DESK

In the entrance pavilion

TOURS

Museum tours are offered for individuals on a walk-in basis at select times. Tours for school and community groups are available by appointment. To request a tour schedule or make an appointment, call 202-633-4646.

MUSEUM STORE

African jewelry, textiles, sculpture, musical recordings, books, exhibition catalogs, posters, and postcards are for sale.

PARTNERS PROGRAM

Partner with the National Museum of African Art! Donate and join the community at africa.si.edu/support.

Above: The north side of the Arts and Industries Building with the Kathrine Dulin Folger

900 Jefferson Drive, SW
(next to the
Smithsonian Castle).
Closed for renovation.
Metrorail:
Smithsonian station.
Smithsonian
information:
202-633-1000
si.edu

ARTS AND INDUSTRIES
BUILDING

If you could step into the Arts and Industries Building, located just east of the Castle, you'd be transported back to 1881. The building opened that year in time for President James Garfield's inaugural ball. Over the years, the Arts and Industries Building has housed and shown many popular objects and exhibitions, from the first ladies' gowns to the *Spirit of St. Louis* and the long-running "1876: A Centennial Exhibition."

The three main halls of the Arts and Industries Building have housed a variety of large-scale changing exhibitions on art, history, science, and culture. The building is currently closed in preparation for renovation.

Above: Willem de Kooning (1904–1997), *Woman, Sag Harbor* (detail), 1964, oil and charcoal on wood
© The Willem de Kooning Foundation/ARS, New York. Opposite top: Claes Oldenburg (b. 1929), *7-Up,*
1961, enamel on plaster-soaked cloth on wire © Claes Oldenburg

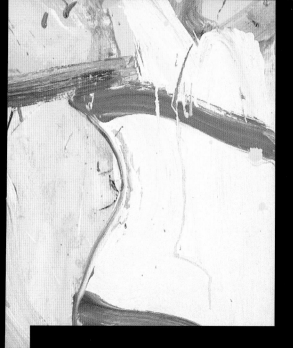

HIRSHHORN MUSEUM AND SCULPTURE GARDEN

Independence Avenue at 7th Street, SW. Building and Plaza entered from Independence Avenue; Plaza and Sculpture Garden entered from National Mall. Open daily. Building, 10 A.M. to 5:30 P.M.; Plaza, 7:30 A.M. to 5:30 P.M.; Sculpture Garden, 7:30 A.M. to dusk. Closed December 25. Metrorail: L'Enfant Plaza station. Smithsonian information: 202-633-1000 hirshhorn.si.edu

This strikingly designed museum of modern and contemporary art is named after the dedicated and enthusiastic American art collector Joseph H. Hirshhorn (1899–1981). His gifts and bequest to the nation of more than 12,000 works are the nucleus of a dynamic collection that remains current through purchases and gifts from many donors. When the museum opened in 1974, the Smithsonian offered, for the first time, a history of modern art in a building and sunken garden that were bold, even daring, by contemporary architectural standards.

Today, the museum is for many the most challenging and visually stimulating of the Institution's attractions on the National Mall. Museum-goers may be dazzled or perplexed by what is on view.

Top: David Smith (1906–1965), *Cubi XII*, 1963, stainless steel.
© Estate of David Smith/Licensed by VAGA, NY.
Above: Mark di Suvero (b. 1933), *Are Years What? (for Marianne Moore)*, 1967, steel and paint. © Mark di Suvero/Spacetime C.C.
Right: Constantin Brancusi (1876–1957), *Torso of a Young Man*, 1924, bronze on stone and wood base.
© Constantin Brancusi/ARS, NY.

but the experience is seldom boring. Art, especially new art, can evoke powerful responses.

A PLACE FOR SCULPTURE . . .

Sculpture was a special passion of the museum's founding donor, and the Hirshhorn's sculpture collection is one of the most distinguished in the world. Sculptures by international artists can be seen throughout the museum, alongside the paintings or in mini-surveys along window walls overlooking the fountain, as well as amid the greenery of the outdoor fountain plaza and along pathways of the Garden. There, adjacent to the National Mall, are several signature works: Auguste Rodin's figure ensemble, *The Burghers of Calais* of 1884–89; compositions by mid-century sculptural giants Henry Moore and David Smith; and the definitive, soaring red steel construction by Mark di Suvero, *Are Years What? (for Marianne Moore)*, 1967, to name a few. Closer to the museum itself, contemporary sculpture is the keynote: here, with the building hovering above, are Juan Muñoz's bronze figures resembling ventriloquists' dummies, *Last Conversation Piece*, 1994–95, and Tony Smith's minimal yet intricate *Throwback*, 1976–79, among others.

. . . AND THE ART OF OUR TIME

Joseph Hirshhorn was dedicated to the art and artists of his time. As he tended to purchase many pieces by artists he particularly admired, the museum is able to present in-depth explorations of such groundbreaking figures as Alexander Calder, Willem de Kooning, and Clyfford Still.

Continuing in Joseph Hirshhorn's tradition, the museum remains committed to acquiring and exhibiting work by emerging and established contemporary artists. Recent acquisition galleries feature the latest pieces to enter the collection and have included such visitor favorites as Ann Hamilton's intriguing installation containing beeswax tablets and live snails, *palimpsest*, 1989, and Ron Mueck's *Untitled (Big Man)*, 2000.

The museum, which screens works by artists and filmmakers from around the world, highlights the growing importance of film and video as artistic mediums. Moving-image exhibitions and film series have long been key parts of the Hirshhorn's program. In 2012,

the museum collaborated with Doug Aitken to present his 360-degree projection *SONG 1* on the building's facade. Aitken created the colorful, moving-image piece with the Hirshhorn's unique architecture in mind. Similarly, Barbara Kruger designed her text-based work *Belief+Doubt,* 2012, as an installation for the museum's shop and lower-level lobby. The Hirshhorn will continue to engage contemporary artists to create spaces that push boundaries and offer visitors experiences that inspire.

Rotating collection exhibitions on all levels of the museum demonstrate the diversity of styles, subjects, and media pursued by an international mix of artists. They have focused on such concepts as sculptors and their drawings, form and formlessness, and repetition of materials and imagery. In addition, important

Top: **Barbara Kruger (b. 1945),** *Belief+Doubt,* **2012, installation in Hirshhorn's lower-level lobby. © Barbara Kruger. Photo by Cathy Carver. Bottom: Doug Aitken (b. 1968),** *SONG 1,* **2012, video projected on the exterior of the museum. Joseph H. Hirshhorn Bequest Fund and Anonymous Gift, 2012, dedicated in honor of Kerry Brougher's service to the Hirshhorn Museum and Sculpture Garden. © Doug Aitken.**

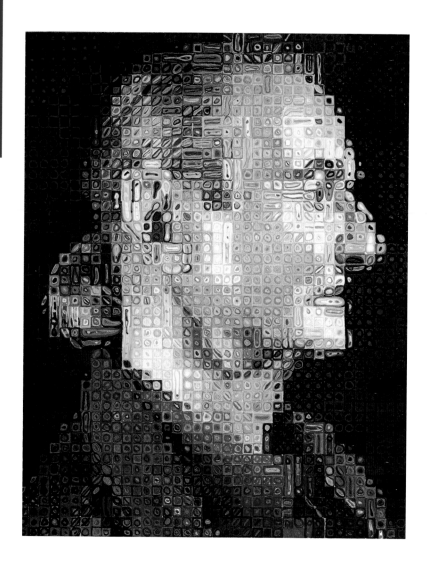

Above: Chuck Close (b. 1940), *Roy II,* 1994, oil on canvas. © Chuck Close/Courtesy of Pace Gallery. Opposite: Georgia O'Keeffe (1887–1986), *Goat's Horn with Red,* 1945, pastel on paperboard mounted on paperboard. © Georgia O'Keeffe/ARS, NY.

monographic and thematic special exhibitions fill the second-level galleries. This dynamic array of presentations offers fresh contexts for exploring modern and contemporary art as well as new ways of looking at the museum's diverse holdings. The galleries on each level continually present a blend of familiar masterpieces and innovative recent works that are sure to intrigue and engage newcomers as well as frequent visitors to the Hirshhorn.

LOOK, LEARN, CREATE

The Hirshhorn offers a range of educational experiences for young and old alike, including lectures and tours by artists and curators, independent film series, informative tours of the permanent collection, and an array of programs, workshops, and activities. Serving visitors with all levels of interest in modern and contemporary art through conversation and dialogue-based tours, Gallery Guides work to engage visitors in open discussions about art. ARTLAB+ workshops for teens connect youth with local artists to investigate current exhibitions at the museum through art-making (see p. 34), and the ARTWORKS program,

designed for teachers, highlights the intersections between contemporary art and learning in the classroom. Providing support at the school, district, and county levels, ARTWORKS aims to shift the national conversation on education to include arts-based learning experiences for all students.

The popular Meet the Artist series, begun in 2000, brings notable artists from around the world to Washington for lectures and discussions about their creative process and recent work. Speakers have included

As the Smithsonian's showcase for modern and contemporary art, the Hirshhorn Museum and Sculpture Garden provides a comprehensive look at art from the first stirrings of modernism in the 19th century to the most recent developments in the art world. Sculpture by modern masters (much of it situated outdoors), international modernist works of the postwar era, and contemporary art are particular attractions. American and European Cubism, Social Realism, Surrealism, Geometric Abstraction, and Expressionism trace modern art past the mid-20th century. Contemporary currents range from Pop art of the 1960s to recent explorations by emerging artists working in a variety of media.

such influential figures as Marina Abramovic, John Baldessari, Matthew Barney, Ernesto Neto, Lorna Simpson, and Hiroshi Sugimoto. Friday lunchtime talks by artists and staff members provide informal occasions for visitors to learn more about the collection exhibitions. In Conversation talks give visitors the rare opportunity to learn about works in the galleries from the artists themselves or to experience the collection from an artist's perspective, while museum staff offer focused explorations of individual pieces on view.

A BOLD SETTING

Gordon Bunshaft (1909–1990), winner in 1987 of the Pritzker Prize in architecture, designed the Hirshhorn. Redesigns of the Sculpture Garden in 1981 and the Plaza in 1993 increased accessibility and enhanced the placement of sculpture with additional greenery. The dynamic and unorthodox building—82 feet high and 231 feet in diameter—encircles an open courtyard and an asymmetrically placed bronze fountain. The exterior wall is a solid surface, broken only by a window 70 feet long in the third-level Abram Lerner Room, from

Above: Dana Hoey (b. 1966), *Waimea,* 2000, C-print on Fujiflex mounted on plastic panel. © Dana Hoey/Petzel, NY. Left: Ai Weiwei (b. 1957), *Cube Light,* 2008, stainless steel, glass, electrical wiring, and lightbulbs. Joseph H. Hirshhorn Bequest and Purchase Funds, 2012. © Ai Weiwei.

which visitors may enjoy a spectacular view of the National Mall. Floor-to-ceiling windows define the inner core, which overlooks the fountain. Four massive piers elevate the concrete structure above the walled plaza. The recessed garden across Jefferson Drive, with its rectangular reflecting pool, provides a peaceful area for viewing art. Outdoors at the Hirshhorn, benches, shaded areas, and fountainside tables provide attractive spots in which to linger. Please enjoy—but do not touch the sculpture!

Above: Andy Warhol (1928–1987), *Self-Portrait*, 1986, synthetic polymer and silkscreen ink on linen. © The Andy Warhol Foundation for the Visual Arts/ARS, New York.

GENERAL INFORMATION

INFORMATION DESK

Located in the lobby and staffed from 10 A.M. to 4 P.M. daily. Information about exhibitions and events is available here.

GUIDES

Gallery Guides are available to answer questions and spark discussion in the galleries between 10:30 A.M. and 4:30 P.M. (Wednesday through Sunday). The Guides also give tours at 12:30 P.M. most days. Ask for more information at the information desk. Tours for groups with up to 60 participants can be scheduled with four weeks' advance notice. Tours of the Sculpture Garden are available June through October and other times upon request, weather permitting. The Programs De-

partment offers tours in French, Spanish, and German upon request. Sign-language tours in the Sculpture Garden for visitors who are blind or have limited vision are also available with advance scheduling. To contact the department for further information, call 202-633-EDUC (3382).

PUBLIC PROGRAMS

A variety of free films, lectures, symposia, and talks by artists are presented regularly in the Marion and Gustave Ring Auditorium on the lower level. Other programs include gallery talks, workshops for a variety of audiences, family art activities, summer music concerts, and programs for teachers, schools, and community groups. For information, call 202-633-EDUC (3382).

MUSEUM STORE

The museum store offers exhibition catalogs, postcards, books on art, and other items related to the museum's programs.

Top: Martial Raysse (b. 1936), *Made in Japan,* 1964, photomechanical reproductions and mixed media. Gift of Joseph H. Hirshhorn, 1972. © 2015 Martial Raysse/ Artists Rights Society (ARS), New York/ ADAGP, Paris. Bottom: Robert Gober (b. 1954), *Untitled,* 1990, wax, cotton, wood, leather shoe, and human hair. © Robert Gober/Matthew Marks Gallery, NY.

Above: Sorting mail on moving trains, which began after the Civil War, was one of the postal service's great innovations. Opposite top: This badge was worn by a pilot in the Airmail Service, which was in operation from August 12, 1918, to September 1, 1927, during which

2 Massachusetts
Avenue at First
Street, NE
(in the old Washington
City Post Office
Building next to
Union Station).
Open daily from
10 A.M. to 5:30 P.M.
Closed December 25.
Metrorail:
Union Station.
Museum information:
202-633-5550
postalmuseum.si.edu

NATIONAL POSTAL

MUSEUM

We are a migratory people. Our brothers,
our neighbors, our children go away from us
and the means of communication with
them by letter and newspapers is one of the
strongest ties that binds [sic] us together.

Congressman Horace Maynard,
Tennessee, 1859

Mail touches everyone, making the
boundaries of postal history limitless.
America's postal history can be defined
through the use of objects as small as
stamps and as mammoth as airplanes. It
is expressed in heartrending letters from
soldiers on foreign battlefields and
through the explosion of direct-mail
marketing. America's postal service was
the force behind the creation of commercial aviation. It helped push the development of cross-country stagecoach routes

and railroads. It ensured the development and perpetual maintenance of rural roads. The postal service was where thousands of African Americans were first able to obtain government employment. America's postal history is the story of the people who made the service work and those who used it. It is the history of mail and the American people.

The National Postal Museum opened on July 30, 1993. Located on Capitol Hill, the museum is housed in the old City Post Office Building. The building, designed by Daniel Burnham, was built between 1911 and 1914. It is a classic Beaux–Arts style structure that complements its next-door neighbor, the Burnham-designed Union Station. The museum has 35,000 square feet of exhibition space, a research library, a stamp store, and a museum store.

The ornate historic lobby formerly served as the main service area of the City Post Office Building. By the 1970s that part of the building had been modernized to an unrecognizable point, a hodge-podge of Formica and harsh fluorescent lighting. Painstaking renovation begun in 1989 restored every foot of the lobby to its original grandeur. Today, the lobby is the foyer to the National Postal Museum.

BINDING THE NATION

This gallery traces events from colonial times through the 19th century, stressing the importance of written communication in the development of the new nation.

As early as 1673, regular mail was carried between New York and Boston following Indian trails. As co-deputy postmaster for the colonies, Benjamin Franklin played a key role in establishing mail service. After the Revolution, Americans recognized that the postal service, and the news and information it carried, was essential to binding the nation together. By 1800, mail was carried over more than 9,000 miles of postal roads. The challenge of developing mail service over long distances is the central theme of "The Expanding Nation," which chronicles the creation of the Butterfield Overland Mail stagecoach line and the famed Pony Express. An interactive video station invites visitors to create their own postal routes.

Above: Children especially enjoy climbing aboard a replica of a 19th-century mudwagon, a Western-style stagecoach.
Opposite: Revenue stamps were first issued in 1862 and continued after the war. In the early 1870s, they ranged in denomination from one cent to $5,000, like this example, which was approved but never issued.

Above: Concord coaches, such as this one from 1851, could hold up to 12 passengers and the mail. Opposite top: This handstamp was salvaged from the USS *Oklahoma*, which sank at Pearl Harbor in 1941. Opposite bottom: Eddie Gardner wore this helmet when flying for the Airmail Service in 1918 for protection in the open cockpits.

CUSTOMERS AND COMMUNITIES

By the turn of the 20th century the nation's population was expanding, as was mail volume and the need for personal mail delivery. Crowded cities and the requirements of rural Americans inspired the invention of new delivery methods. Facets of the developing system and its important role in the fabric of the nation are explored through photographs, mail vehicles, a variety of rural mailboxes, and other artifacts.

Parcel Post Service helped usher in an era of consumerism by the early 20th century that foreshadowed the massive mechanization and automation of mail and the mail-order industry. Today, mail service is a vital conduit for business.

MOVING THE MAIL

Faced with the challenge of moving the mail quickly, the postal service was constantly on the lookout for the fastest transportation system available, from post riders to stagecoaches, automobiles, and trucks, to trains and airplanes. These various means of transportation are the focus of the museum's atrium gallery.

"Moving the Mail" features three vintage airmail planes, a 1931 Ford Model A postal truck, an 1851 stagecoach, a replica of a railway mail car, and a full-size semi-truck cab cutaway.

After the Civil War, postal officials began to take advantage of trains for moving and sorting the mail. Railway mail clerks worked the mail while it was being carried between towns. In 1918, airmail service was established on a regular basis between New York, Philadelphia, and Washington, DC. Airmail contracts provided funding for the development of the commercial aviation industry.

Visitors will discover the story of Owney, a little stray dog adopted by postal workers in New York. He became the mascot of the Railway Mail Service and traveled thousands of miles across the United States.

MAIL CALL

Personal letters are vivid windows into history. A series of rotating exhibits in this gallery conveys the stories of families and friends who are bound together by letters over distance and across time. A poignant video is the highlight of "Mail Call," which celebrates the bond of mail between soldiers and their loved ones back home.

The National Postal Museum is a family-oriented museum that explores the history of the nation's postal service and celebrates the art of letter writing and the beauty and lore of stamps. Visitors can travel on the first postal road, sit in a stagecoach and a semi-truck cab cutaway, create 19th-century mail routes, and personalize a souvenir postcard. They can also enjoy more than 30 audiovisual and interactive areas. Changing exhibitions focus on philatelic rarities, families and letter writing, individuals featured on US stamps, and more.

WILLIAM H. GROSS STAMP GALLERY

Since Great Britain issued the first adhesive postal stamp in 1840, stamps of every subject, shape, and design have been produced for consumer use or as collectibles. Stamps not only serve as proof of postage but are also miniature works of art, keepsakes, rare treasures, and the workhorses of the automated postal system. Some stamps tell stories, while others contain secrets and hidden meanings.

Stamps from the United States and around the world are on display in the museum's state-of-the-art gallery. Featuring stamps from the museum's vast collections as well as special items from other collections, the gallery offers visitors access to spectacular rarities. Changing philatelic exhibits have featured Franklin D. Roosevelt's stamp sketches, the first US stamps, and the 24-cent inverted Jenny airmail stamp of 1918, possibly the most famous US stamp.

Above: Stamps and other philatelic materials form the core of the museum's collections. Opposite: The Post Office Department promoted its speedy new service with posters in post offices across the country.

grams, films, lectures, performances, and much more. Sign language and oral interpreters for programs and tours require two weeks' advance notice. For more information about upcoming public programs, call 202-633-5533 or visit the museum's Web site.

GENERAL INFORMATION

ENTRANCE

Enter the lobby of the building and proceed by escalator to the floor level of the museum's 90-foot-high atrium.

INFORMATION DESK

Off the lobby

TOURS

Scheduled tours for students and groups of ten or more are available. Reservations for these tours must be made three weeks in advance. For a walk-in tour schedule, or to make reservations for a student or group tour, call 202-633-5535.

PUBLIC PROGRAMS

An array of public programs offer visitors fresh perspectives on mail in their lives. Museum programs include hands-on workshops, interactive family pro-

RESEARCH FACILITIES

With more than 40,000 volumes and manuscripts, the museum's library is among the world's largest facilities for postal history and philatelic research. The library features a specimen study room, an audiovisual viewing room, and a rare book collection. Open by appointment, Monday through Friday from 10 A.M. to 4 P.M.; call 202-633-5543 to schedule a visit.

MUSEUM STORE

Located near the escalators at the museum entrance, the museum store offers posters, T-shirts, stationery, postcards, pins, first-day covers, stamp-collector kits, stamp- and postal-related souvenirs, books for all ages on postal-history subjects and letter collections, and a selection of philatelic publications.

STAMP STORE

Operated by the US Postal Service, the stamp store is located opposite the museum store. Visitors may purchase a variety of current stamps and other commemorative stamp items.

US POST OFFICE

Accessible from the main hall of the museum

Exterior of the Donald W. Reynolds Center for American Art and Portraiture in Washington, DC, home to the Smithsonian's National Portrait Gallery and the Smithsonian American Art Museum. Opposite left: Stuart Davis (1894–1964), *Int'l Surface No. 1*, 1960, oil on canvas. Smithsonian American Art Museum. Opposite right: Tom Wolfe (b. 1931) by Everett Raymond Kinstler, 2000, oil on canvas. National Portrait Gallery; gift of Sheila Wolfe. © 2002 Everett Raymond Kinstler.

DONALD W. REYNOLDS CENTER FOR AMERIC[A]
ART AND PORTRAITURE

TWO AMAZING MUSEUMS. ONE INCREDIBLE PLACE.

The National Portrait Gallery and the Smithsonian American Art Museu[m] located in the heart of downtown Washington, DC. Their National Histo[ric] Landmark building is a dazzling showcase for American art and portraitu[re that] celebrates the vision and creativity of Americans. The museums share a [main] entrance at 8th and F Streets, NW, which provides easy access to current [infor-] mation on special exhibitions, public programs, and other visitor ameniti[es.]

The museums and their specialized new facilities—the Lunder Conser[vation] Center, the Luce Foundation Center for American Art, the Nan Tucker M[cEvoy] Auditorium, and the Robert and Arlene Kogod Courtyard—are known collectively as the Donald W. Reynolds Center for American Art and Port[raiture.]

Robert and Arlene Kogod Courtyard

The Robert and Arlene Kogod Courtyard is enclosed with an elegant glas[s] canopy, a signature element shared by the two museums. It was designe[d by] world-renowned architects Foster + Partners and provides a distinctive, c[ontem-] porary accent to the museums' Greek Revival building.

Lunder Conservation Center

The museums share the innovative Lunder Conservation Center, the first [art] conservation facility with floor-to-ceiling glass windows that allow the pu[blic] permanent behind-the-scenes views of the museums' preservation work. [Visi-] tors can learn about conservation science through educational kiosks, vi[deos,] and public programs.

Above: M. F. K. Fisher (1908–1992) by Ginny Stanford, acrylic on canvas (detail), 1991, acrylic on canvas. © Ginny Stanford. Opposite top: Benjamin Harrison (1833–1901) by an unidentified artist, wood, 1888. Opposite bottom: Barack Obama (b. 1961) by Shepard Fairey. Gift of the Heather and Tony Podesta Collection. © Shepard Fairey (Obe 2)

8th and F Streets, NW.
Open daily from
11:30 A.M. to 7 P.M.
Closed December 25.
Metrorail:
Gallery Place /
Chinatown station.
Museum information:
202-633-8300.
Smithsonian
information:
202-633-1000
npg.si.edu

NATIONAL PORTRAIT GALLERY

Generations of remarkable Americans are kept in the company of their fellow citizens at the National Portrait Gallery. The museum presents the wonderful diversity of individuals who have left and who are still leaving their mark on our country and our culture. Through the visual and performing arts, we feature leaders such as George Washington and Martin Luther King Jr., artists such as Mary Cassatt and George Gershwin, activists such as Sequoyah and Rosa Parks, and icons of pop culture such as Babe Ruth and Marilyn Monroe, among thousands of others. They all link us to our past, our present, and our future. For anyone fascinated by famous Americans and their stories, the National Portrait Gallery is a must-visit destination.

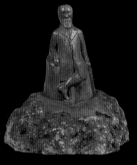

Below: Robert F. Kennedy (1925–1968) by Roy Lichtenstein, 1989, lithograph. Gift of *Time* magazine. © Estate of Roy Lichtenstein. Opposite: George Washington (1732–1799), "Lansdowne" portrait, by Gilbert Stuart, 1796, oil on canvas. Acquired as a gift to the nation through the generosity of the Donald W. Reynolds Foundation.

The Portrait Gallery reopened in 2006 after an extensive six-year renovation of its National Historic Landmark building. The structure itself, begun in 1836 for the US Patent Office, stood for the highest aspirations of the nation. Praised by Walt Whitman as "the noblest of Washington buildings," it was saved from the wrecking ball in 1958 and then welcomed the opening of the National Portrait Gallery in 1968. That was no accident. Pierre L'Enfant, in his design for the new federal city, had envisioned for this site a place to honor the nation's heroes. In our own time, a building has been reborn and a vision fulfilled.

Portraiture as an art form is alive across the United States. In several exhibitions each year, the National Portrait Gallery showcases new talent and new faces. Every three years, the Outwin Boochever Portrait

Competition invites artists to submit their work to be considered for entrance into the exhibition, cash prizes, and the top prize of executing a commission of a remarkable living American for the museum. In "Portraiture Now," the museum continues a new series of exhibitions featuring contemporary artists who explore with imagination and skill the age-old art of depicting the figure. Through paintings, sculpture, photographs, drawings, and video art, artists bring compelling figurative art into the 21st century.

One of the building's most popular exhibitions is "America's Presidents," the nation's only complete collection of presidential portraits outside the White House. This exhibition lies at the heart of the Portrait Gallery's mission to tell the country's history through the individuals who have shaped it. Visitors can see an enhanced and extended display of multiple images of 43 presidents of the United States, including Gilbert Stuart's

"Lansdowne" portrait of George Washington, the
famous "cracked-plate" photograph of Abraham
Lincoln, and whimsical sculptures of Lyndon Johnson,
Jimmy Carter, Richard Nixon, and George H. W. Bush
by noted caricaturist Pat Oliphant.

Maya Angelou by Ross Rossin (b. 1964), 2013, oil on canvas. Gift of Andrew J. Young Foundation. © Ross R. Rossin.

Presidents Washington, Andrew Jackson, Lincoln, Theodore Roosevelt, and Franklin D. Roosevelt are given expanded attention because of their significant impact on the office.

Located adjacent to "America's Presidents," "The Struggle for Justice" showcases individuals from the museum's permanent collection who played significant roles in advancing civil rights and justice. The installation includes a range of activists from Frederick Douglass and Susan B. Anthony to Martin Luther King, Jr. and Cesar Chavez, all whom struggled on behalf of disenfranchised Americans.

A "conversation about America" is on view in a series of 17 galleries and alcoves entitled "American Origins," which is chronologically arranged to take the visitor from the days of first contact between Native Americans and European explorers, through the struggles of independence, to the Gilded Age. Major figures include Pocahontas, Alexander Hamilton, Henry Clay, Nathaniel Hawthorne, and Harriet Beecher Stowe.

Three galleries devoted to the Civil War—"Faces of Discord"—examine this conflict in depth. A selection of modern photographic prints produced from Mathew Brady's original negatives complements the exhibition. Highlights from the Portrait Gallery's remarkable collection of daguerreotypes (the earliest practical form of photography) make the National Portrait Gallery the first major museum to create a permanent exhibition space for daguerreotype portraits.

Each year, a gallery within the museum called "One Life" is devoted to a single curator's exploration of the life of an individual.

Four newly created galleries opening onto the museum's magnificent third-floor Great Hall showcase the major cultural, scientific, and political figures of the 20th century, including cultural icon Marilyn Monroe. From the reform movements of the first two decades to the movements for social justice and civil rights of the 1950s, 1960s, and 1970s, and from the Great Depression to the Vietnam era and beyond, visitors can experience the people who defined the decades of that century.

Two exhibitions on the third-floor mezzanines highlight particular themes in American life. "Bravo!" features individuals who have brought the performing arts to life, from the late

Fred Astaire (1899–1987) by Edward Steichen, 1927, gelatin silver print. Acquired in memory of Agnes and Eugene Meyer through the generosity of Katharine Graham and the New York Community Trust, The Island Fund. Permisssion of Joanna T. Steichen © The Estate of Edward Steichen.

AT A GLANCE

Through the visual, performing, literary, and electronic arts, the National Portrait Gallery provides a stage for remarkable Americans to share their stories with us. Highlights from the museum's collections include Gilbert Stuart's "Lansdowne" painting of George Washington, perhaps the most significant portrait in America's history, as well as exhibitions on the presidents, paintings, photographs, and drawings.

Abraham Lincoln by Alexander Gardner (1821–1882), 1865, albumen silver print.

19th century through the present. "Champions" salutes the dynamic American sports figures whose impact has extended beyond the athletic realm and made them a part of the larger story of the nation. Every three years, the National Portrait Gallery invites artists from across the nation to participate in the Outwin Boochever Portrait Competition. The portrait competition and exhibition encourage artists to explore the art of portraiture by submitting works they have created. The events celebrate excellence and innovation, with a strong focus on the variety of portrait media used by artists today.

In October 2014, the Portrait Gallery created "Recognize" as an opportunity for people to decide what will go on display as the museum continues to acknowledge those who have influenced American politics, history, and culture. The museum's historians and curators select three portraits that highlight an influential person in the collection, and the winner is elected by fans of the Portrait Gallery who can vote online through Smithsonianmag.com.

Rosa Parks (1913–2005)
by Marshall D. Rumbaugh,
1983, limewood.

So far, voters have chosen the portraits of artist Georgia O'Keeffe, comedian George Carlin, and baseball Hall of Famer Roberto Clemente to be installed on the "Recognize" wall.

The National Portrait Gallery has a lively selection of public programs that use art as a vehicle to introduce individuals in the collection along with their significant contributions to American society. The department develops innovative, thoughtful programming for visitors from near and far. Using the exhibitions as a catalyst for these educational offerings, the collections come alive through interactive school tours, docent tours, and programming. For offerings during your visit, check the museum's Web site.

Above: Edward Hopper (1882–1967), *Cape Cod Morning* (detail), 1950, oil on canvas.

Opposite top: Malcah Zeldis (b. 1931), *Miss Liberty Celebration*, 1987, oil on corrugated

cardboard. Gift of Herbert Waide Hemphill, Jr. © 1987, Malcah Zeldis. Opposite bottom:

Robert Reid (1862–1929), *The Mirror,* about 1910, oil on canvas. Gift of William T. Evans.

8th and F Streets, NW.
Open daily from
11:30 A.M. to 7 P.M.
Closed December 25.
Metrorail:
Gallery Place /
Chinatown station.
202-633-7970.
Museum information:
202-275-1500
Smithsonian
information:
202-633-1000.
americanart.si.edu

SMITHSONIAN
AMERICAN
ART MUSEUM

The Smithsonian American Art Museum,
the nation's first collection of American
art, is an unparalleled record of the
American experience. The collection
captures the aspirations, character, and
imagination of the American people over
three centuries.

   More than 7,000 artists are represented
in the museum's collection, including
masters such as John Singleton Copley,
Winslow Homer, John Singer Sargent,
Mary Cassatt, Georgia O'Keeffe, Edward
Hopper, Jacob Lawrence, David Hockney,
Lee Friedlander, Nam June Paik, Martin
Puryear, and Robert Rauschenberg.
Artworks in the collection reveal key
aspects of America's rich artistic and
cultural history from the colonial period
to today. The museum's historic Greek

Georgia O'Keeffe (1887–1986), *Manhattan*, 1932, oil on canvas. Gift of the Georgia O'Keeffe Foundation.

Revival building was meticulously renovated in 2006 with expanded permanent collection galleries and the Luce Foundation Center for American Art, the first visible art storage and study center in Washington.

The museum has been a leader in collecting and exhibiting the finest works of American art. Pioneering collections include media art and video games; photography from its origins in the 19th century to contemporary works; images of western expansion; realist art from the first half of the 20th century; historic and contemporary folk art; and work by African American and Latino artists. The museum has the largest collection of New Deal art and murals, and the largest collection of American sculpture.

LUCE FOUNDATION CENTER FOR AMERICAN ART

The Luce Foundation Center, the first visible art study and storage center in Washington, provides new ways to experience American art with more than 3,300 artworks from the museum's collection on display. It features paintings densely hung on screens; sculptures, craftworks, and folk art objects arranged on shelves; and portrait miniatures, bronze medals, and jewelry in drawers that slide open with the touch of a button. Interpretive materials and artist biographies are available for every work.

As a major center for research in American art, the museum includes such resources as the Inventory of American Paintings executed before 1914, with data on nearly 290,000 works; the Peter A. Juley & Sons collection of 127,000 historic photographs; the Pre-1877 Art Exhibition Catalog Index; the Inventory of American Sculpture, with information on more than 85,000 indoor and outdoor works; and the Joseph Cornell Study Center.

Lily Furedi (1932–2006), *Subway*, 1934, oil on canvas. Transfer from the US Department of the Interior, National Park Service.

Above: William H. Johnson
(1901–1970), *Café*, about
1939–40, oil on paperboard.
Gift of the Harmon Foundation. Opposite above: Nam
June Paik (1932–2006),
*Electronic Superhighway:
Continental U.S., Alaska,
Hawaii*, 1995, 51 channel
video installation (including
one closed-circuit television feed), custom electron-
ics, neon lighting, steel, and
wood; color, sound. Gift of
the artist. © Nam June Paik
Estate. Opposite: George
Catlin (1796–1872),
*Buffalo Bull's Back Fat,
Head chief, Blood Tribe*,
1832, oil on canvas.

COLLECTIONS

The Smithsonian American Art Museum's collection
tells the story of America through the visual arts.
Colonial portraiture, 19th-century landscapes,
American Impressionism, 20th-century realism
and abstraction, New Deal projects, sculpture,
photography, prints and drawings, African American
art, Latino art, folk art, and media art are featured in
the collection. Contemporary American crafts are
presented at the Smithsonian American Art
Museum's Renwick Gallery (see p. 195).

Two early Puerto Rican wood sculptures, *Santa
Barbara* from about 1680 to 1690 and *Nuestra Señora
de los Dolores (Our Lady of Sorrows)* from about 1675
to 1725, are the oldest works in the collection. Colonial
America is represented with portraits by John
Singleton Copley, Charles Willson Peale, and Gilbert
Stuart, landscapes by Thomas Cole, and sculptures by
Horatio Greenough.

AT A GLANCE

The nation's first American art collection comprises more than 300 years of painting, sculpture, media art, photography, graphic art, and folk art. The museum's historic Greek Revival building in the heart of the nation's capital has been meticulously renovated with expanded permanent collection galleries and the Luce Foundation Center for American Art, the first visible art storage and study center in Washington. A wide array of free public programs are offered; visit americanart.si.edu for information.

For decades, the museum championed the artists who captured the spirit of the frontier and the lure of the West. George Catlin, Frederic Remington, Thomas Moran, and Albert Bierstadt celebrated the landscape and paid tribute to Native Americans and their cultures.

The museum has one of the finest and largest collections of American Impressionist paintings and artwork from the last quarter of the 19th century, a period dubbed the "Gilded Age" by author Mark Twain. Artists included are Childe Hassam, Mary Cassatt, William Merritt Chase, Winslow Homer, John Singer Sargent, and James McNeill Whistler.

The country's largest collection of New Deal art and murals can also be found at the Smithsonian American Art Museum. Realist painters include Edward Hopper, John Sloan, and Andrew Wyeth.

Some American modernists, like Georgia O'Keeffe and Joseph Stella, captured the spirit of their age with inventive new ways of depicting the world, while artists such as Willem de Kooning and Franz Kline created wholly abstract compositions. Other important 20th-century painters in the collection are Marsden Hartley, Stuart Davis, Wayne Thiebaud, Alfred Jensen, and Philip Guston.

In recent years, the museum has focused on acquiring major works by modern and contemporary artists, including Oscar Bluemner, Christo, Nancy Graves, David Hockney, Jenny Holzer, Edward and Nancy Kienholz, Liz Larner, Roy Lichtenstein, Nam June Paik, Martin Puryear, and James Rosenquist.

The museum's sculpture collection, ranging from works by 19th-century masters Horatio Greenough, Harriet Hosmer, Edmonia Lewis, and Augustus Saint-Gaudens to renowned 20th-century artists Louise Nevelson, Isamu Noguchi, and Edward Kienholz, is the largest collection of American sculpture anywhere. Works on paper comprise a large part of the collection, notably prints from the 20th century and more than 150 years of photography.

The Smithsonian American Art Museum also has a long tradition of championing works that initially did not have a place in the story of American art. The museum was one of the first museums to collect and display folk art in its galleries. In the last decade, it has acquired almost 500 pieces of Latino art, spanning colonial times to today.

Extensive holdings by William H. Johnson are part of the museum's notable collection of more than 2,000 artworks by African American artists. Other African American artists represented include Romare Bearden, Robert Scott Duncanson, Sam Gilliam, Louis Mailou Jones, Jacob Lawrence, and Henry Ossawa Tanner.

The Lincoln Gallery, Smithsonian American Art Museum.

GENERAL INFORMATION
(For Portrait Gallery and American Art)

BUILDING HISTORY

The National Portrait Gallery and the Smithsonian American Art Museum share a National Historic Landmark building located in the heart of Washington, DC's vibrant downtown. A recent renovation (2000–2006) has restored exceptional architectural features, such as porticoes modeled on the Parthenon, a graceful curving double staircase, colonnades, vaulted galleries illuminated by natural light, and skylights as long as a city block.

Modern enhancements, such as the Lunder Conservation Center and the Kogod Courtyard, honor the forward-thinking ideas and American ingenuity that have flourished in the building from its early days as the nation's Patent Office. The building is now a dazzling showcase for art and portraiture that celebrates the vision and creativity of Americans.

Begun in 1836 and completed in 1868, the Patent Office Building is one of the oldest public buildings constructed in early Washington. Several important early American architects were involved in the original design of the building, preeminently Robert Mills (1781–1855). It is considered one of the finest examples of Greek Revival architecture in the United States.

Patent models, the government's historical, scientific, and art collections, including the Declaration of Independence and George Washington's Revolutionary War camp tent, were displayed on the third floor. During the Civil War, the building was used as a temporary military hospital and barracks. In March 1865, it was the site of President Abraham Lincoln's inaugural ball.

In the 1950s, the building was scheduled for demolition, but the nascent historic preservation movement successfully campaigned to save it. Congress transferred the building to the Smithsonian in 1958, and the museums opened to the public in the building in 1968.

INFORMATION DESK

Located in the lobby

TOURS

Walk-in tours with museum docents are offered. For information on group tours, call 202-633-1000.

PUBLIC PROGRAMS

Free public programs include gallery talks, films, illustrated lectures, artist workshops, family days, and performances of music, dance, and theater. For information call 202-633-1000 or visit npg.si.edu and americanart.si.edu.

MUSEUM STORE

The museum stores on the first floor feature collection-inspired gifts, note cards, posters, books, calendars, jewelry, and more.

CAFÉ

The Courtyard Café offers casual dining with a seasonal menu of America-

inspired dishes. It is open from 11:30 A.M. to 4 P.M.; coffee, beer and wine, and light fare are available until 6:30 P.M.

WI-FI

Free public wireless Internet access (Wi-Fi) is available throughout the building. Stay connected with the National Portrait Gallery through the Web (npg.si.edu); Facebook; Instagram (@smithsoniannpg); a blog (face2face.si.edu); Twitter (@npg); and YouTube (youtube.com/NatlPortraitGallery).

Opposite: Luce Foundation Center for American Art. Below: Robert and Arlene Kogod Courtyard.

Above: Albert Paley (b. 1944), *Portal Gates,* 1974, forged steel, brass, copper, and bronze. Opposite top: Joshua Demonte (b. 1984), *Curtains and Balcony Bracelet,* 2008, 33 percent glass-filled polyamide. Gift of Irene and Bob Sinclair. © 2008 Joshua DeMonte

Pennsylvania Avenue at
17th Street, NW.
Open daily from
10 A.M. to 5:30 P.M.
Closed December 25.
Metrorail: Farragut
West station
(17th Street exit).
Smithsonian
information:
202-633-1000.
Museum information:
202-633-7970.
americanart.si.edu

RENWICK GALLERY OF
THE SMITHSONIAN
AMERICAN ART MUSEUM

The Renwick Gallery, a branch of the
Smithsonian American Art Museum, is
dedicated to the future of art. It exhibits
the most exciting works by American
craft artists who are taking both traditional and innovative approaches to their
materials and continually expanding the
definitions of craft and art. The building,
a national historic landmark named in
honor of its architect, James Renwick Jr.,
has been home to the museum's contemporary craft program since 1972. The
permanent collections galleries on the
second floor emphasize a philosophy of
craft as a way of living differently in the
modern world through extraordinary
handmade objects, while the first- floor
galleries host special rotating exhibitions
and installations. Artists represented in
the Renwick Gallery collection include
Vivian Beer, Wendell Castle, Nick Cave,

AT A GLANCE

Changing exhibitions of American crafts and decorative arts— historic and contemporary as well as selections from the permanent collection of 20th- and 21st-century American crafts— are on view in this distinguished building. The building was the first purpose-built museum in America, designed to showcase the art and cultural achievements of the still-new nation.

Dale Chihuly, Mary Jackson, Karen LaMonte, Albert Paley, Ken Price, Lenore Tawney, Peter Voulkos, and many others.

The collection has always strongly emphasized contemporary work, although special exhibitions

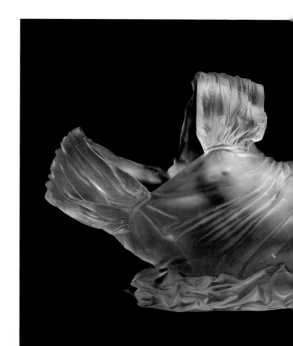

sometimes feature historical traditions to trace the evolution of craft movements. The works on view showcase artists who have a genius for working with materials in inventive ways that transform our everyday world. The Grand Salon, a 4,300-square-foot gallery with a soaring 38-foot ceiling, is considered one of Washington's premier interior spaces.

BUILDING HISTORY

The Renwick Gallery building was constructed in 1859 to house the art collection of William Wilson Corcoran, a prominent Washington philanthropist and banker. It was the first purpose-built art museum in America, a symbol of the nation's aspirations for distinctive cultural achievements. Corcoran engaged the noted architect James Renwick Jr., who had earlier designed the Smithsonian's Castle and St. Patrick's Cathedral in New York City. Renwick modeled the gallery in a French style that was first used in the pavilions of the Musée du Louvre, and he added distinctly American touches. When Corcoran's museum opened, it was considered one of the most elegant buildings in the country and hailed as the

Opposite: Ken Price (1935–2012), *Inez*, 2010, fired and painted ceramic. Gift of the James F. Dicke Family, © 2010, Ken Price, Inc. Below: Karen LaMonte (b. 1967), *Reclining Dress Impression with Drapery*, 2009, glass. Gift of the James Renwick Alliance and Colleen and John Kotelly, © 2009, Karen LaMonte.

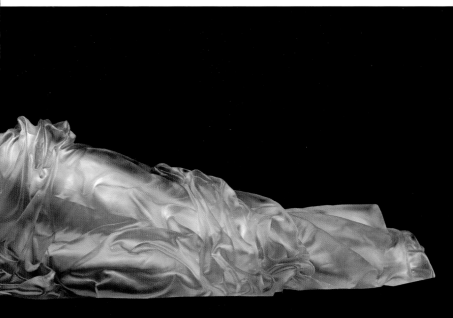

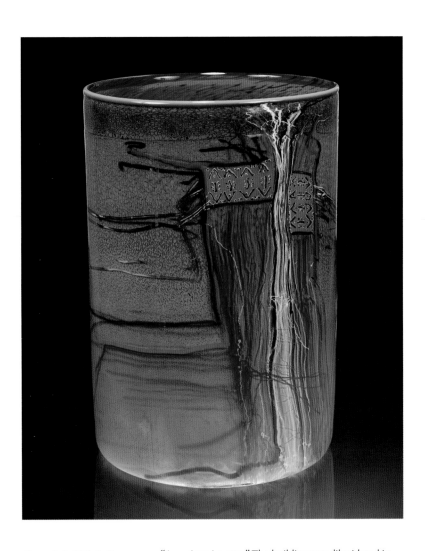

Above: Dale Chihuly (b. 1941), *Blanket Cylinder Series*, 1984, blown glass. Gift of Eleanor T. and Samuel J. Rosenfeld, © 1984, Dale Chihuly. Opposite: Wayne Higby (b. 1943), *Temple's Gates Pass*, 1988, hand-built, raku-fired, and glazed earthenware. © 1988, Wayne Higby.

"American Louvre." The building was dilapidated in the early 1960s and a proposal was made to tear it down, but First Lady Jackie Kennedy led the effort to save the architectural gem. In 1965, the gallery was turned over to the Smithsonian. Subsequently dedicated "for use as a gallery of art, crafts and design" and then extensively renovated, the Renwick building reopened in 1972 as the home of the Smithsonian American Art Museum's contemporary craft program. Four decades later, the Smithsonian American Art Museum again refurbished the Renwick Gallery, to preserve its historical integrity and modernize it to

meet the needs of a 21st-century museum. The Renwick reopened in November 2015 with a completely renewed infrastructure, enhanced historical features, upgraded technology, and a fresh, dynamic presentation of its permanent collection and new acquisitions.

GENERAL INFORMATION

INFORMATION DESK
In the lobby

TOURS
Walk-in tours with museum docents are offered. Group tours must be arranged in advance by calling 202-633-8550.

PUBLIC PROGRAMS
Free public programs include craft demonstrations, gallery talks, films, and illustrated lectures. For information, call 202-633-1000 or visit american art.si.edu.

MUSEUM STORE
The museum store features Renwick publications and other craft and decorative art books, craft objects relating to exhibitions, postcards, note cards, holiday cards, posters, calendars, and jewelry.

MEMBERSHIP
Become a member of the Smithsonian American Art Museum and enjoy special benefits including a discount in Smithsonian stores. For more information, call the membership office at 202-633-6362 or visit americanart.si.edu.

Above: Untitled, glass beads sewn on fabric, 2014, Ubuhle Artists, a South African women's collective promoting empowerment through art. Opposite above: Guitar of Chuck Brown (1936-2012), the "Godfather of Go Go" featured in the exhibition "Twelve Years that Shook and Shaped Washington: 1963-1975."

1901 Fort Place, SE.
Open daily from
10 A.M. to 5 P.M.
Closed December 25.
Metrorail:
Anacostia station.
Smithsonian
Information:
202-633-1000
Museum information:
202-633-4820
anacostia.si.edu

ANACOSTIA
COMMUNITY MUSEUM

Current, Connected, Compelling
The Anacostia Community Museum
enhances the understanding of
contemporary urban life through its
innovative community-based approach
to research, exhibitions and public
programming. Building upon more
than four decades of work in history
and culture, the museum explores and
documents how people engage, shape,
respond and confront contemporary
issues. The museum addresses universal
themes of empowerment, neighborhood
change, and globalization through an
examination of community history and
cultural traditions; growth, economic
and environmental impacts; interaction
between diverse communities and the
arts and creativity.

AT A GLANCE

The Anacostia Community Museum was established in 1967 as the nation's first federally funded neighborhood museum. It evolved into a significant resource focused on issues of contemporary urban life as an outgrowth of its earlier African American history mission. With this foundation, research, exhibitions, and public programs have expanded.

Scholars and researchers continue to find unique opportunities to use the excellent research facilities at the Anacostia Community Museum. The museum's collection of archival materials, photographs, books, and artifacts reflect neighborhood and city history, women's history, literature, family history and African American studies. A major research thrust is the Community Documentation Project which records the history and changes in the local urban community and is the basis for broader national and internal issues addressed in exhibitions and programs under the museum's expanded direction. Just as the research, collection development and outreach are models for replication by other community-oriented museums so are the museum's public programs. Through the more than 100 programs held annually, the museum offers further interpretation of exhibitions on view, expands on research and collections topics, presents music and other performance-based programs, youth and family programs.

GENERAL INFORMATION

HOW TO GET THERE

The Anacostia Museum is located in historic Fort Stanton Park in southeast Washington, DC, with ample parking for cars and buses.

By Metrorail and Metrobus: Take the Green Line to the Anacostia station and transfer to the W-2 or W-3 Metrobus to the museum. *By car:* From downtown, take the southeast Freeway (I-395) to the 11th Street Bridge and exit onto Martin Luther King Jr. Avenue. At the fourth traffic light, turn left at Morris Road and drive up the hill to the museum on the right. *From I-295 south:* Take the Howard Road exit and turn left on Howard Road. Travel to Martin Luther King Jr. Avenue and turn left. Turn right at Morris Road and continue up the hill to the museum. Visit anacostia.si.edu for more information on the spring/summer shuttle Anacostia service.

INFORMATION DESK

In the entrance lobby

SPECIAL ACTIVITIES AND TOURS

Special activities for adults and children include lectures, workshops, films, and performances. A calendar of events is available on request. For information about exhibitions and programs or to schedule a tour, call 202-633-4844. Visit the museum's Web site at anacostia.si.edu for more information, or to subscribe to e-communications, follow the museum on Facebook and Twitter.

Programs for adults, families, and youth include lectures, workshops, films and performances. A print calendar of events is available on request. For subscription to the e-calendar and other e-communication, visit anacostia.si.edu. For information about exhibitions and programs or to schedule a tour, call 202-633-4844. Follow the museum on Facebook, Twitter, and Instagram.

RESEARCH

The museum's Research Department provides fellowship and internship opportunities to undergraduate and graduate students in public history, community-oriented studies, and African American studies. Internships are also available in the Collections, Design and Production, Education, Special Events, and Public Affairs departments. For more information about internships, call 202-633-4838 or e-mail reinckenss@si.edu.

Above: The diary of the formerly enslaved 19th-century patriarch Adam Francis Plummer is featured in the exhibition "Hand of Freedom: The Life and Legacy of the Plummer Family," 2015. Opposite: "How the Civil War Changes Washington," 2015, examines the evolution of the capital city, contextualizing its history and significant events with intriguing stories of some individuals who came here and contributed to the city's growth.

Above: The Zoo's male giant panda rests in his habitat. Opposite top: The National Zoo is working to save the Bali mynah from extinction. Opposite bottom: The Zoo's main pedestrian entrance is located on Connecticut Avenue.

NATIONAL ZOOLOGICAL PARK

Entrances: Connecticut
Avenue, NW (3001 block
between Cathedral Avenue
and Devonshire Place);
Harvard Street and Adams
Mill Road intersection;
Beach Drive in
Rock Creek Park.
Open daily
see page 223 for hours.
Closed December 25.
Metrorail:
Woodley Park/Zoo/
Adams Morgan station
or Cleveland Park station.
Recorded information
and Information Desk:
202-633-4888.
nationalzoo.si.edu

The National Zoo is known internationally for the exhibiting, breeding, and study of wild animals. Most of the Zoo's animals live in naturalistic settings that comfortably house social groups resembling those found in the wild.

Vertebrate species, representing the most spectacular and familiar forms of land animals, make up the most visible part of the collection, but invertebrate and aquatic species provide a more comprehensive picture of animal life. Educational graphics and demonstrations including daily programs, animal training and enrichment, feeding, and keeper talks supplement public understanding of the park's animals and plants.

Native and ornamental plants grow throughout the 163-acre park. The butterfly garden (featuring plants that attract

butterflies) provides living examples of the interaction among plants, animals, and humans. Olmsted Walk, the central path, connects the major animal exhibits. It is named for the father of landscape architecture, Frederick Law Olmsted, who created the original design for the National Zoo as well as the US Capitol grounds, the Washington National Cathedral grounds, and New York's Central Park.

EXHIBITS

The giant pandas occupy the top spot on the Zoo's "must see" list. The pandas' state-of-the-art habitat is designed to mimic the pandas' natural habitat of rocky, lush terrain in China. Each element has a purpose—from helping the pandas stay cool in hot weather to giving them a place to hide when they need privacy. Rock and tree structures are perfect for climbing, and grottoes, pools, and streams for keeping cool.

The pandas are the gateway to the Asia Trail— nearly six acres of exhibits featuring endangered or threatened Asian species. Joining giant pandas along the Trail are clouded leopards, fishing cats, Asian

Top: The world's largest lizard, the Komodo dragon, uses its tongue to explore its environment. Bottom: The brilliantly colored green tree pythons are a favorite in the Zoo's Reptile Discovery Center.

small-clawed otters, Japanese giant salamanders, red pandas, and sloth bears.

Along the American Trail, guests can wander through landscaped paths and discover unparalleled opportunities to come face-to-face with California sea lions and gray seals, watch playful beavers and otters, admire the classic beauty of eagles and wolves, and splash and play in a kid-friendly seasonal tide pool. American Trail showcases species that are gems of North American wildlife and treasures to us all. The animals here represent the triumph of the American spirit and success stories in conservation.

Asian elephants are critically endangered; fewer than 50,000 remain in their native countries. The National Zoo is committed to their conservation and to the powerful connection made when visitors experience the magnificence of elephants in the Zoo.

At Elephant Trails, visitors experience the sights, sounds, and smells of being close to the Zoo's Asian elephants. In addition, interactive exhibits teach visitors about elephants' physical characteristics, social behaviors, and intelligence and the commitment it takes to care for them at the Zoo.

Elephant Trails spans 8,943 square meters, which is large enough to accommodate up to three separate groups of elephants, including a natural, matriarchal herd and individual bulls. Altogether, the facility can house between eight and ten adult Asian elephants and their young.

At the Reptile Discovery Center, visitors can explore the biology of reptiles and amphibians. Visitors may use listening, visual, and olfactory skills to investigate how "herptiles" feed and communicate. Afterward, they can apply their knowledge to living animals, which include alligator turtles, king cobras, tentacled snakes, alligators, gavials, and Komodo dragons. The Reptile Discovery Center is located in the former Reptile House. Fantastical carved reptiles, sculpted doors, and columns at its main entrance decorate the facade of this Romanesque building which, when it opened in 1931, was recognized

by the American Institute of Architects as the outstanding brick building in the eastern United States. In the Small Mammal House, come face-to-face with the sprightly grace of the golden lion tamarin, the uncanny armor of the three-banded armadillo, and the fascinating quills of the prehensile-tailed porcupine. Gaze at naked

mole rats as they move from chamber to chamber, and observe the tamandua—an arboreal anteater—searching in logs for its favorite treats: mealworms. Catch a glimpse of rare animals that were on the verge of extinction like the black-footed ferret, or see something native to your own backyard such as the striped skunk.

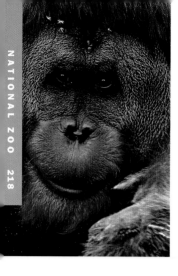

Think Tank introduces visitors to the science of animal cognition. Thinking ability in animals is presented through the topics of tool use, language, and society. Orangutans, hermit crabs, Norway rats, as well as computers and games stimulate exploration. Orangutans can move between the Think Tank and their Great Ape House enclosures, several hundred feet farther along Olmsted Walk, by swinging, or brachiating, across the Orangutan Transport System. This series of towers connected by heavy cables allows orangutans to move as they would in their heavily forested, tropical homes.

Great Cats is home territory for some of the visitors' favorite animals: lions and tigers.

A walk through Amazonia introduces visitors to the high degree of biological diversity in a tropical rain forest. The 15,000-square-foot rain forest habitat of the exhibit includes a 55,000-gallon

Top: Several of the National Zoo's orangutans participate in a computer-based language project at Think Tank. Bottom: The National Zoo's gorilla family gives visitors insights into the great ape's behavior and social structure. Opposite: Sumatran tigers, extremely rare in the wild, are ambassadors for the Zoo's conservation and science initiatives.

aquarium for the display of Amazon River fish. Within Amazonia's dome, visitors find a living tropical forest with more than 350 species of plants, including 50-foot-tall trees, tropical vines, and epiphytes. This habitat is also home to species of mammals, birds, and insects typical of the Amazon Basin, all moving throughout the exhibit.

The "Amazonia Science Gallery" is an 8,000-square-foot experimental science education/outreach center that brings visitors into the day-to-day world of scientific research and the people who do it. The "Amazonia Science Gallery" includes Amphibian Alert!—a hands-on exhibit—featuring more than 15 species of frogs and other amphibians, including the extinct-in-the-wild Panamanian golden frog. Through

close-up animal views and interactive exhibits, visitors discover what's threatening these amphibian "jewels" and what's being done to save them. Science On a Sphere (SOS) is a state-of-the-art exhibit created by the National Oceanic and Atmospheric Administration. SOS effectively illustrates Earth System science to people of all ages.

The Visitor Center, near the Connecticut Avenue entrance, has an auditorium, souvenir shop, and restrooms.

CONSERVATION AND RESEARCH

What the visitor sees at the National Zoo reveals only a small part of the Zoo's complexity as a scientific

research organization. National Zoo scientists, working on the grounds in Washington, DC, and at the 3,200-acre Smithsonian Conservation Biology Institute in Front Royal, Virginia, were among the founders of the field of conservation biology. National Zoo scientists continue as leaders today, with global perspectives and long-term experience in conducting zoo- and field-based research. Their discoveries enhance the survival or recovery of species and their habitats, helping to ensure the health and well-being of animals in zoos and their counterparts in the wild. The National Zoo is also a global leader in training the next generation of conservation and zoo professionals through undergraduate, graduate, and professional education that emphasizes well-founded approaches to conservation.

The National Zoo's Cheetah Conservation Station allows visitors to see this endangered cat in a naturalistic habitat that encourages behavior typical to that observed in the wild.

HISTORY

Although the Smithsonian Institution received gifts of live animals almost from its beginning, there was no zoo to house and study the living collection. Some of

the animals were sent to zoos elsewhere; some were kept on the National Mall. Over the years, a sizable menagerie accumulated outside the Smithsonian Castle. In 1889, Congress established the National Zoological Park at the urging of Samuel Pierpont Langley, third Secretary of the Smithsonian, and William T. Hornaday, a Smithsonian naturalist who was particularly concerned about the looming extinction of the American bison. Six bison were among the animals transferred from the Mall to the National Zoo when the grounds opened in 1891.

Animal collecting expeditions in the early 1900s, together with gifts from individuals and foreign governments and exchanges with other zoos, augmented the Zoo's population and introduced Washingtonians to rare and exotic animals, including the Tasmanian wolf (now extinct), bongo, and Komodo dragon.

Today, the National Zoo continues to develop a bond between humans and animals

Above: A male Panamanian gold frog at the National Zoo is part of a Species Survival Plan. Below: The sunbathing seals attract visitors to the Zoo's American Trail.

Scimitar-hared oryx can be seen in the Zoo's Cheetah Conservation Station. Below: The National Zoo is one of the few places outside New Zealand where people can observe a live kiwi. The Zoo has successfully bred these unique birds.

that helps visitors understand biology and scientific concepts that will guide them in making informed choices in daily life. Exhibits, educational programs, school programs, training opportunities, and public lectures all bring the rich diversity of life on Earth to a variety of local, national, and international audiences. In the 21st century, the Zoo's mission is to provide leadership in animal care science, conservation, and public education.

FRIENDS OF THE NATIONAL ZOO

Friends of the National Zoo (FONZ) is a nonprofit, membership-based organization dedicated to supporting the conservation, education, and science mission of the Smithsonian's National Zoo. Since 1958, FONZ has supported the Zoo by implementing education, membership and volunteer programs, hosting special events, raising funds for Zoo projects, and providing guest services for Zoo visitors and grants to Zoo scientists.

To learn more about FONZ programs and membership options, visit fonz.org.

GENERAL INFORMATION

HOW TO GET THERE

The Zoo is accessible from the Woodley Park/Zoo/Adams Morgan and Cleveland Park Metrorail stations and is accessible by Metrobus. For Metro information, call 202-637-7000 or check the Web site wmata.com. Limited pay parking is available on Zoo lots. Bus-passenger discharge and pickup and limited free bus parking are available.

HOURS (unless otherwise posted)

April–October: Animal exhibits are open from 10 A.M. to 6 P.M. every day. November–March: Animal exhibits are open from 10 A.M. to 4:30 P.M. every day. The Zoo is open every day except December 25.

TOURS

Guided weekend highlight tours of the Zoo for families, individuals, or groups are available with an eight-week advance reservation. Call Friends of the National Zoo at 202-633-3025.

SERVICES

The Zoo has ramped building entrances and restroom facilities for visitors with disabilities. Strollers may be rented in season for a small fee. A limited number of wheelchairs are available to rent. Zoo police provide lost-and-found service and a refuge for lost children.

WHERE TO EAT

The Zoo has a variety of fast-food facilities. Picnic areas are located throughout the grounds, but no outdoor cooking is permitted.

GIFT SHOPS

Unique zoo-oriented souvenirs, postcards, books, T-shirts, and art objects are for sale.

FEEDING TIMES

Check at the information desks for feeding times and demonstrations.

HELPFUL HINTS

Consider using public transportation. Zoo parking lots often fill up early in the warm months. Wear comfortable clothing and shoes. During the warmer months, visit early in the day or in the evening, when the park is less crowded and the animals are more active. Fall and early winter are great times to visit the Zoo. For more information, visit nationalzoo.si.edu.

SOME RULES TO FOLLOW

Pets, except certified assistance animals, are not permitted in the park. The area between the guardrail and the enclosure barrier is for your safety and that of the animals. Stay on your side of the guardrail. Zoo animals are wild and easily excited. Do not feed or attempt to touch the animals. The Zoo provides excellent, balanced diets, and additional feeding is unhealthy for them. Do not skate or ride bicycles in the park. Radios and other audio devices must be used with earphones.

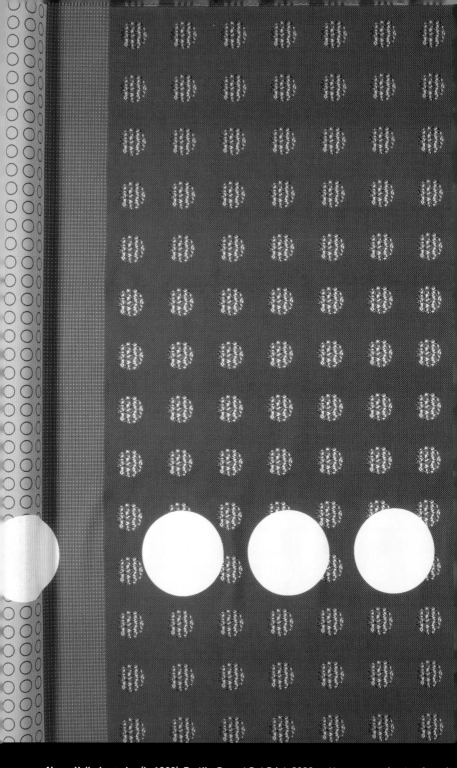

Above: Hella Jongerius (b. 1963), Textile, Repeat Dot Print, 2002, cotton, rayon, polyester. Opposite top: Michael Eden (b. 1955), designer, Tall Green Bloom Urn, England, 2012, 3-D printed nylon. Mus

COOPER HEWITT,
SMITHSONIAN
DESIGN MUSEUM

2 East 91st Street
(at Fifth Avenue),
New York City.
Open weekdays and
Sundays, 10 A.M. to
6 P.M.; Saturdays,
10 A.M. to 9 P.M.
Closed Thanksgiving
and December 25.
Admission fee.
Pay What You Wish,
Saturdays,
6 P.M. to 9 P.M.
212-849-8400
cooperhewitt.org

Founded in 1897, Cooper Hewitt is the only museum in the nation devoted exclusively to historic and contemporary design. In 2014, Cooper Hewitt reopened in the renovated and restored Andrew Carnegie Mansion with 60 percent more exhibition space than it had previously and a completely reimagined visitor experience. Interactive galleries throughout the museum's four floors now encourage visitors to explore the collection digitally on ultra-high-definition touch-screen tables, draw their own designs in the Immersion Room, and engage in the design process in the dynamic Process Lab.

Technology is a key element of the reinvigorated museum, which has been a branch of the Smithsonian since 1967. The interactive Pen—a global first— transforms the museum experience, allowing visitors to collect, create, and permanently save their visits.

EXHIBITIONS

Cooper Hewitt's galleries present unique temporary exhibitions as well as installations drawn from the permanent collection.

Located on the museum's first floor, the Nancy and Edwin Marks Gallery presents the popular, ongoing "Selects" series, which invites prominent designers, artists, and architects to mine and interpret the museum's collection to curate their own unique exhibitions. Guest curators have included the Ghanaian British architect David Adjaye, best-selling author and artist Maira Kalman, and Dutch textile designer Hella Jongerius.

The entire second floor is dedicated to showcasing objects from the museum's permanent collection. Here, the Models & Prototypes Gallery, provides insights into the important role of architectural models and design prototypes in the design process. Featured objects have included 18th- and 19th-century staircase models and 20th-century car models and drawings. The former Carnegie Family Library on the second floor displays intricately ornamental teak woodwork created by Lockwood de Forest.

The new 6,000-square-foot Barbara and Morton Mandel Design Gallery on the third floor features exhibitions organized by curatorial staff and guest curators that juxtapose the historic and the contemporary.

Frank O. Gehry (b. 1929), designer, Bubbles Chaise Longue, USA, ca. 1988, layered and bent corrugated cardboard.

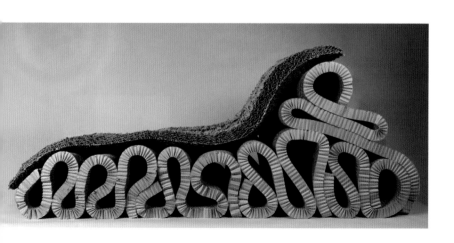

DESIGN TRIENNIAL

Cooper Hewitt's renowned "Triennial" exhibition series was launched in 2000 to critical acclaim. The only exhibition of its kind in the country, it showcases some of the most exciting, provocative, and innovative design created around the globe during the previous three years. The Triennial presents work from emerging talent and established designers in the fields of fashion, architecture, graphics, digital media, and furniture.

COLLECTIONS

Cooper Hewitt's four curatorial departments (Drawings, Prints, and Graphic Design; Product Design and Decorative Arts; Textiles; and Wallcoverings) oversee one of the most diverse design collections in existence: more than 210,000 objects that span 30 centuries. The core collection was formed between the late 19th and early 20th century by the museum's founders, Sarah and Eleanor Hewitt, who conceived it as a "practical working laboratory," a "visual library"

Installation view of **"Making Design."**

Van Cleef and Arpels and Junichi Hakose (b. 1955), Araiso U brooch, France and Japan, 2007, raised white gold, gold beads, eggshell lacquer on mother-of-pearl support on white gold, round-cut diamonds.

**Top: Sidewall, USA,
1920–30, machine-
printed on paper.
Opposite top:** *Feathers,*
**Alexander Girard
(American), 1957.
Opposite bottom: Chair,
Charles Eames
(American), 1944.**

where students and designers could be inspired by actual objects. In addition to furniture, metalwork, glass, ceramics, jewelry, woodwork, textiles, and wallcoverings, the museum has one of the largest collections of drawings and prints in the United States, spanning the fields of architecture, advertising, fashion, theater, and interior design. The thrust of the collection has always been history, innovation, process, technique, use, and social context more than masterpieces. The current collecting focus has shifted to contemporary objects, bolstering the American holdings, and acquiring major historical pieces.

With a focus on educating, inspiring, and empowering people through design, Cooper Hewitt offers exhibitions, educational programming, digital initiatives, and an on-site master's program, all of which explore the process of historic and contemporary design. The museum's four floors occupy the landmark Andrew Carnegie Mansion on Museum Mile in New York City. The grounds include the Arthur Ross Terrace and Garden, the city's largest private garden.

GENERAL INFORMATION

VISITOR SERVICES

Just inside the main entrance

TOURS

Private and self-guided tours for groups of ten or more are available by reservation at 212-849-8351; public tours, offered twice daily, are free with admission.

SHOP COOPER HEWITT

The SHOP features significant design objects from around the world and focuses on American designers. Offerings reflect the museum's design philosophy, mission, and collection and include items related to current exhibitions.

CAFÉ

Cooper Hewitt's café offers a seasonal menu and a variety of coffees, pastries, and artisanal wines. Seating is available indoors and outdoors in the adjoining Arthur Ross Terrace and Garden. Like the garden, the café is open to the public, free of charge, beginning at 8:00 A.M. weekdays.

EDUCATIONAL PROGRAMS

Cooper Hewitt's extensive educational programs include activities for all ages, from public lectures to hands-on workshops. Design in the Classroom introduces thinking about design to underserved schoolchildren in New York City and across the nation, and Design Field Trips bring students into the museum to explore current exhibitions. In association with Parsons School of Design, the museum also offers an on-site master's program in the history of design and curatorial studies.

SMITHSONIAN DESIGN LIBRARY

The Smithsonian Design Library's 90,000 volumes—including 10,000 rare books on ornament, architecture, and decorative arts—is an unparalleled resource for design and decorative arts materials from the Renaissance to the present. The library is open by appointment.

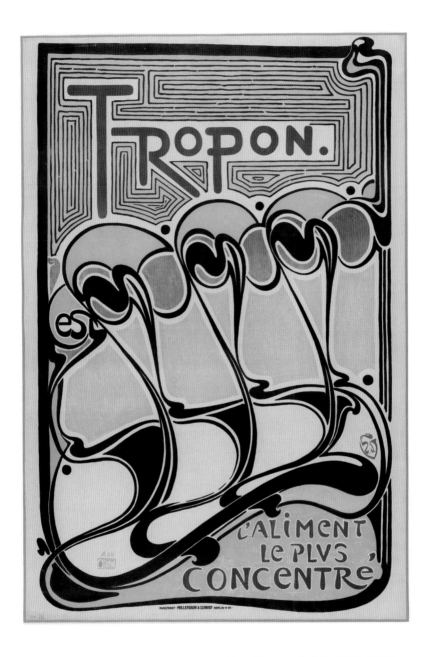

Above: Henry van de Velde (1863–1957), designer, *Tropon est l'aliment le plus concentre,* 1898, lithograph on wove paper, lined. Opposite: *Ladies' Old Shoes,* Plate IX, T. Watson Greig, Edinburgh, Scotland, 1885.

SMITHSONIAN ACROSS AMERICA

The Smithsonian's commitment to reach Americans beyond Washington, DC, has never been stronger. New collaborations are taking shape between the Smithsonian and museums, cultural and educational organizations, and communities across the nation. The Smithsonian's national programs offer a variety of traveling exhibits, educational workshops, cultural presentations, and partnership opportunities, all of which can be tailored and combined to meet the needs of organizations and communities across America. Visit the Smithsonian Across America Web site, saa.si.edu, to view a calendar of Smithsonian exhibitions and programs taking place in your state. Four Smithsonian units work together to achieve this national outreach mission; they are described on the following pages.

SONIA SOTOMAYOR
Her Remarkable Journey
to the Supreme Court

Supreme Court Justices Sonia Sotomayor (shown), Ruth Bader Ginsburg, and Antonin Scalia are among the distinguished guests presented by the Smithsonian Associates. Noted authors, scientists, historians, sports personalities, and cultural figures are also in the spotlight at public programs. Preceding pages: Smithsonian Summer Camp, a program of the Smithsonian Associates, provides one-of-a-kind learning experiences that spark the imagination and create plenty of fun. National Smithsonian Associates programs for teachers and students bring the Smithsonian's world of knowledge into classrooms across the country.

THE SMITHSONIAN ASSOCIATES

The Smithsonian Associates, established in 1965, offers access to the Smithsonian's world of knowledge through innovative, engaging programming that promotes learning, enrichment, and creativity for people of all ages.

The largest museum-based educational program in the world, the Smithsonian Associates annually offers more than 750 lectures, performances, studio art classes, and study tours to its members and the general public.

Performances at Discovery Theater, museum sleepovers, and more than 90 educationally focused summer camps foster the joys of learning for young people and their families, and offer them a gateway to the Smithsonian's rich array of museums and resources.

Teachers and students across the country make the Smithsonian part of their classrooms through the Smithsonian Associates' extensive national education outreach program, which brings Smithsonian-designed content and experts to a wide range of partnering museums and other community sites.

In partnership with George Mason University, a master of arts degree program in the history of decorative arts provides training for the next generation of curators, design specialists, and researchers.

For more information about the Smithsonian Associates' programs or membership opportunities, call 202-633-3030 or visit smithsonianassociates.org.

SMITHSONIAN AFFILIATIONS

Smithsonian Affiliations is a national outreach program that develops long-term, high-quality partnerships with museums and educational organizations to share collections, exhibitions, learning opportunities, and research expertise. Each year more than 20 million visitors to affiliated organizations experience the Smithsonian in their neighborhoods, where they have

In the image, partial text is visible:

Smithsonian Instit
Affiliations Progra

This artifact on loan fr
National Air a
Space Museu

the opportunity to view major works of art, historic spacecraft, natural specimens, and icons of American history. Beyond offering exhibits and artifacts, Smithsonian Affiliations reaches across the nation to provide educational programs for K–12 students and adult learners. Smithsonian Affiliations also collaborates with partner organizations on membership and marketing. For more information regarding Smithsonian Affiliations, call 202-633-5300 or visit affiliations.si.edu.

Visitors at the San Diego Air & Space Museum, a Smithsonian Affiliate, view the Apollo 9 space capsule, on loan from the Smithsonian's National Air and Space Museum.

SMITHSONIAN CENTER FOR LEARNING AND DIGITAL ACCESS

The Smithsonian Center for Learning and Digital Access produces and delivers Smithsonian educational experiences, services, and products informed by research and Smithsonian expertise and collections. Focusing on the needs of teachers and students, it collaborates with other educational organizations,

Students create an exhibit using Smithsonian-based learning techniques.

especially to offer professional development. The Center's Web site, *Smithsonian Learning Lab,* is an engaging digital destination for educators and learners of all abilities to discover, create, and share resources and ideas while developing knowledge and skills critical for academic and professional success. To explore this inspiring learning environment and to contact the Center, visit learninglab.si.edu.

SMITHSONIAN INSTITUTION TRAVELING EXHIBITION SERVICE

The Smithsonian Institution Traveling Exhibition Service (SITES) has been sharing the wealth of Smithsonian collections and research programs with millions of people outside Washington, DC, for more than 65 years. SITES connects Americans to their shared cultural heritage through a wide range of exhibitions about art, science, and history. Exhibitions are shown not only in museums but also wherever people live, work, and play: in libraries, science centers, historical societies, community centers, botanical gardens, schools, and shopping malls. Exhibition descriptions and tour schedules are available on the Web. For more information, call 202-633-3168 or visit sites.si.edu.

Below: "Titanoboa: Monster Snake," an exhibition that examines the discovery of a prehistoric 48-foot long, 2,500-pound snake is touring museums nationwide.

SMITHSONIAN INSTITUTION MEMBERSHIPS

The Smithsonian invites people of all ages across the country and around the world to become Associate members. You may choose from an exciting array of membership programs. The benefits of each membership program are described below.

NATIONAL ASSOCIATE MEMBERSHIP

For members nationwide and worldwide, open to all.

SMITHSONIAN MAGAZINE (11 ISSUES) The largest cultural magazine in the country with top-notch writing and captivating photographs; it illuminates history, science, nature, travel, and the arts.

AMENITIES IN WASHINGTON, DC A cordial welcome and special information materials at the museum information desks

DISCOUNTS at Smithsonian Museum Stores (excluding the National Zoo and the separately administered National Gallery of Art), online at smithsonianstore.com, and with Smithsonian Catalog

• 10 percent off meal purchases at select Smithsonian dining facilities, and reduced rates on tickets to the Smithsonian's IMAX® theaters and planetarium

• Special reduced member rates on Smithsonian Folkways Recordings purchased at folkways.si.edu and on limited-edition art through the Smithsonian Associates Art Collectors Program.

For more information, call 1-800-766-2149 or visit smithsonian.com.

SMITHSONIAN REGIONAL EVENTS Invitations to special events occurring in your metropolitan area

MEMBERS ONLY TRAVEL Eligibility for Smithsonian travel programs across the country and around the world with Smithsonian Journeys

FREE ADMISSION. No charge for members visiting the Cooper Hewitt, Smithsonian Design Museum in New York City

SMITHSONIAN ASSOCIATES MEMBERSHIP

Membership in the largest museum-based educational program in the world includes these benefits:

DISCOUNTS of 25 to 40 percent on most of the more than 750 lectures, courses, performances, studio arts classes,

Smithsonian Associates' Discovery Theater presents programs in Smithsonian museums, such as sessions on flight at the Air and Space Museum.

and local and regional study tours offered annually.

MEMBERS-ONLY TICKET PRIORITY for most programs.

A SUBSCRIPTION TO *SMITHSONIAN ASSOCIATES*, a monthly program guide.

DISCOUNTS for Smithsonian museum shops, the Smithsonian catalog, SmithsonianStore.com, and select Smithsonian restaurants, as well as on purchases of Smithsonian Folkways recordings and fine-art prints from the Art Collectors Program.

INVITATIONS to members-only programs and events, such as the annual Breakfast at the Zoo, private tours, and gallery visits.

OPPORTUNITIES for volunteer service. For more information, call 202-633-3030 or visit smithsonianassociates.org.

FRIENDS OF THE SMITHSONIAN CONTRIBUTING MEMBERSHIP & JAMES SMITHSON SOCIETY

Those who join the Friends of the Smithsonian Contributing Membership and the James Smithson Society, its highest membership group, help shape the Smithsonian's collection, preservation, education, and research efforts through their generous philanthropic support. While all members receive National Associate benefits, additional exclusive benefits commensurate with each member level are also awarded, including:

GIFT EDITIONS of current Smithsonian books and recordings; the exquisite annual Smithsonian desk calendar and guidebook; and the Smithsonian's annual report.

RECEPTIONS AND BEHIND-THE-SCENES TOURS of the newest exhibitions and venues;

DEEP DISCOUNTS at Smithsonian stores, selected Smithsonian dining facilities, Smithsonian IMAX® theaters, Smithsonian catalog purchases, and on Folkways recordings.

Opposite: The Smithsonian Castle, in the heart of the nation's capital

JAMES SMITHSON SOCIETY members enjoy exclusive receptions, behind-the-scenes tours, the *Food for Thought* summer luncheon series, and, each spring, the Annual Smithsonian Weekend, culminating in a black-tie gala.

CHARITABLE-GIFT TAX DEDUCTIONS BASED ON LEVEL OF MEMBERSHIP For more information, call 1-800-931-3226 or e-mail membership@si.edu.

AIR & SPACE ASSOCIATE MEMBERSHIP

For enthusiasts of aviation, space flight, and modern technology. Membership includes the following benefits:

***AIR & SPACE* MAGAZINE (6 ISSUES)** Chronicles the history, culture, and technology of flight and space exploration

For more information, call 1-800-513-3081 or visit airandspacemag.com.

AMENITIES IN WASHINGTON, DC A cordial welcome and special information materials at the museum information desks

DISCOUNTS at Smithsonian Museum Stores (excluding the National Zoo and the separately administered National Gallery of Art), online at smithsonianstore.com, and with Smithsonian Catalog.

▪ 10 percent off meal purchases at select Smithsonian dining facilities and reduced rates on tickets to the Smithsonian's IMAX® theaters and planetarium

For more information, call 1-800-766-2149 or visit airandspacemag.com.

SMITHSONIAN REGIONAL EVENTS Invitations to special events occurring in your metropolitan area.

MEMBERS-ONLY TRAVEL Eligibility for Smithsonian travel programs across the country and around the world with Smithsonian Journeys

FREE ADMISSION No charge for members visiting the Cooper Hewitt, Smithsonian Design Museum in New York City

One of 12 lunar modules built for Project Apollo, "LM2" in the National Air and Space Museum was used for drop tests in Earth's atmosphere.

REYNOLDS CENTER
AMERICAN ART MUSEUM

METRO CENTER **M**

PORTRAIT GALLERY

TO RENWICK GALLERY
▼ *10-minute walk from American History*

15TH STREET

14TH STREET

12TH STREET

10TH STREET

9TH STREET

CONSTITUTION AVENUE

AFRICAN
AMERICAN

AMERICAN
HISTORY

NATURAL HISTORY

MADISON DRIVE

WASHINGTON
MONUMENT

14TH STREET

THE CASTLE
Smithsonian Visitor Center

SMITHSONIAN
M

JEFFERSON DRIVE
RIPLEY CENTER*

FREER
GALLERY

ARTS AND
INDUSTRIES
(CLOSED FOR RENOVATION)

HIRSHH

INDEPENDENCE AVENUE

SACKLER
GALLERY*

AFRICAN
ART*

C STREET

D STREET